The Legendary Red Dog

A Book of Tails

A Collection of "Tails"
My Life and Travels On The Road

BY: JOSEPH L. "RED DOG" CAMPBELL

Copyright © 2001 Joseph L. "Red Dog" Campbell.
All rights reserved. No part of this book may be used
or reproduced in any manner whatsoever without
the express written consent of the author, except for
up to two paragraphs for review purposes only.

FIRST EDITION, 2001, 1,000 copies
FIRST EDITION REPRINT, 1,000 copies
SECOND EDITION, 2010, 500 copies
THIRD EDITION, 2017, 250+ copies

Forward

NOBODY HANDLES SUCCESS, SUCCESS HANDLES THEM. With that in mind I'll repeat the little saying Gregg said to me one day. With fame comes separation. And I'll add one to it, not destructtion. Fame gives you the opportunity to grow and to expand separately. Or if you are a group, to grow as a group. Success beats you down and you start believing the bullshit. So until you get past thinking you are someone you are not, success will handle you. When you learn that, and everyone in the business eventually learns it or they are gone, you are able to just go with it and enjoy the fruits of your labor.

I think that Cameron Crowe wrote one of the best articles, or perhaps the best article that has ever been written about the Allman Brothers Band. It's almost as good as my tails, and I say that with a laugh at my own style. When you add the fact that he was only fifteen, that just makes it incredible. You can see why he's at the top of his field. I do thank you Cameron for putting my character in your movie Almost Famous. I say that from my heart. You put a tear in my eye. I guess you can say it does pay to be nice to people.

I wear my own shoes on this, and didn't ask the Brothers for help, comments, or for comments from anyone else to help sell the book. Nor did they offer, I leave that up to you, the reader.

This was put together from start to finish by myself, a couple friends, and Chuck Wehmeyer. I wrote the book in 1994 and in 2001 asked them to help me edit and put the book out. These are my words, my responsibility, and we are not professional publicshers. I didn't go to a publishing house because they give you x number of dollars and they're the ones who get fat. That's saying it real simple. I think you get the point. So, with that in mind I say, "I was born a poor man, I'm a poor man now, and I'll more than likely die a poor man." I also hope you understand when I say, I would like to get the full benefit of my hard work, sink or swim. This is for my retirement, and that's as straight forward as I can put it to you.

I wrote this book as if I were standing on the corner busting some tails with my partners. My tails won't come at you in any order. I hope in reading them you'll pick up on that, and don't look at the mistakes. Just clear your mind and enjoy the stories....

Red Dog

This book is dedicated to all the people who get off their asses and go to work every day.

And to my grandad, Tully S. Hobbs

Learning to Swim

Brother Duane always said I'd be the one to write the book, so here I am. Today is the day I start, Wednesday, May 6, 1994. It's a misty and cloudy day, and I'm just sitting back looking at my life.

"Life seems to be a big trap with a bunch of little traps," is what brother Berry Oakley used to say. "You fall in one trap, then you finally work your way out, take two steps, and bang! You fall in another one." As I look back, I realize how Brother Berry's philosophy still rings true even 27 years later.

So, here I sit trying to pull myself out of a trap I've been in for five years. I've just been told to take a year off and get things together, things in my life that come out a little later in my tails. That's why I'm writing. It's the best way I know to get them out. Sit down and write this book.

My name is Joseph Lawrence Campbell. Better known as Red Dog. Some people say the Legendary Red Dog. Well, I didn't know I was legendary. I was born in Tampa, Florida on March 27, 1942, the son of Joe Lilious Campbell and Sarah Lucile Hobbs. My mother was born in Dublin, Georgia, and my father in Sylvester, Georgia.

Mom had the responsibility of raising three kids: my sister Phyllis, who was about eight years old at the time; my brother Richard, who was one; and the "Red-headed Terror of Riverview Terrace," me — that was my first nickname.

I was an honest and straightforward kid — something that carries over even to this day. I don't think you can find anyone who would ever say I ripped them off or that I wasn't honest and up front. I remember growing up in a hellhole; a rough, low rent project called Riverview Terrace in Tampa, Florida. Every walk of life lived there, and if you wanted to keep your marbles; you better believe you had to be tough — tough and ready to fight. I fit right in too. Or better yet, I learned to fit in.

I was one of those kids that you had to kick my ass if you wanted my shit. I wasn't about to give my marbles up to anyone. Like the time Tommy, who always tried to act tough, came up and said he was going to take my shooter. Not this week! Bam! I hit him right in the kisser. Never had trouble from him or anybody else after that. You better believe I went home with my marbles every night. Hell, I didn't dare go home and say, "So and so took my marbles." My mom and my dad, if he were even there, would have sent my young ass right back out the door. Then I had better come back with my marbles or else!

The reason I say, "if my dad were there," is because my parents were separated. They divorced when I was young. My mom remarried when I was about five. She married a man named Owen R. Coile. Owen was one hell of a good man, and that's what my dad said: "If he can stay with your mother, he's a good man."

That's because my mom is what I call a fiery woman. She says what's on her mind, and doesn't care who she is talking to. She is also one hell of a hard worker. During the wars with Germany and Japan she did what all the other ladies of the country did. They worked their asses off doing whatever they could to help the county while the men were off fighting the wars. They also had the pressure of putting food on the table for their children.

Both my dad and Owen were in the Navy. My dad got out after the wars and Owen stayed in until he was medically discharged after 27 years of service. He lost his vocal chords to cancer. My dad and his brother, my Uncle Tom, owned a good size dairy in Tampa. I loved my dad to death. He was my hero. I used to love to go places and do things with him. I remember he used to get up at four in the morning to go milk the cows, and I would wake up a little later — around five. He would go to work and I would play while he was working. I used to like to ride in the feed barrel, a wheel barrel full of feed, while he shoveled feed into the troughs.

There was this big open field that ran from the house to the barn, and the field was full of sandspurs. Every morning when I went across the field to see my dad my feet would get loaded with sandspurs. And every time I'd be out there crying, he'd come and get me. But, that was okay because I was with him.

A little while later we sold the dairy and my dad and Uncle Tom went down to Marathon, Florida to build houses. I remember they also had some deal going with a big ol' barge moored out in the gulf. Man, I really loved to be with him. On Sundays he would swim out to the barge and do some repair work or check on something. Then he would swim on back to shore. Well, this barge is about 100 yards off shore, and since I couldn't swim, he made me stay on shore until he got back. On this one Sunday, my dad tells me to stay on the beach and wait for him. What he didn't know was that I'd already had an earlier idea of what swimming was about.

Around this time we lived in an upstairs apartment over a small grocery store. Hell, there was only one grocery store in town with two apartments upstairs and my Uncle Tom lived in the other one. One day about a month before this particular Sunday, I was out behind the house fishing from the dock with my sister Phyllis and my brother Richard. We were fishing, and I'm just about to drop my line in when a big old barracuda swims by. You know; razor sharp teeth — take your arm off in a second and you don't even know until a few seconds later.

Now the gulf is pretty clear in a lot of places. In some spots you can even see the bottom. You can wade out and stand ankle deep in water that gradually drops off with each step until all of the sudden it drops straight down, maybe ten or 12 feet. So like I said, I'm getting ready to let my drop line in when this barracuda swims by, so I wait up a couple seconds and then go ahead. I drop my line off the dock and start fishing, but for some reason, I get an idea to reach down and try to grab the string. Well, no way — splash! — there I go, head first in the water. Where I fell in just happened to be one of those spots where the water was already over my head, and believe me, all I could think about was this barracuda coming back around to get me.

Now I remembered seeing people swim. I remembered seeing them move their arms and kick their legs, so I went into gear, moving everything just as fast as I could. Kicking my legs and flailing my arms, and somehow I managed to swim about eight feet back to the dock. When I finally reached the dock, I grabbed on to one of those pillars which supports the dock, then I see there's a damn crab about five feet away. I start crying and crying because I think the crab is going to get me. Well, I struggle to climb back up on the dock, hustle my stuff together, get my net and head off. Most of all now I know I can swim. I have confidence.

For a month after that, every day I would go down to what we called our swimming pool. A little pool in the gulf enclosed by cement walls. It was really just a plain old cement wall in the water. A cement wall with three sides and holes covered by wire so the fish couldn't get in, only the water could. Well, I'd swim from ladder to ladder right next to the wall; hugging it and learning a little more each time, teaching myself how to swim. Swimming by fire. That's the way I've done a lot of things, and I've always come out on top.

Now I told you my dad was my hero. Where he went, I wanted to go. On this one particular Sunday, he strips down to his swimsuit and starts swimming to the barge. Out through the water, which is loaded with sharks and barracuda. Well, old "Red Bird," was what he called me, was right behind him. He heard me, looks over, and there I was! I could see he was a little worried because of the sharks, but I also saw a lot of pride in him that day. That's when I became his favorite of the boys. He knew I would try to do anything and nothing seemed to scare me. Nothing except for those damn crabs that is.

So you see, it's like I said earlier, like Brother Berry used to say, "Life seems to be a big trap with a bunch of little traps. You fall in one trap, then you finally work your way out, take two steps, and bang! You fall in another one." You just have to keep climbing out.

When my mom married Owen, we moved to Jacksonville, Florida where he was stationed. We lived there and in Norfolk, Virginia, before moving to Lexington Park, Maryland, where I attended Great Mills High School. I was 16 when I joined the Lexington Park Volunteer Fire Department. I was in the Junior Auxiliary. When I turned 18, I was voted into the Senior Department. The next month I was elected Second Lieutenant and three months later I was elected First Lieutenant, fourth in command, which carried a lot of responsibility. Not only around the firehouse, but also at school. I was the senior fireman of all the firemen attending high school. During a fire or a fire drill the firemen were in charge of the school, the students, the teachers, and the principal; Miss Jane. That made me the head dog, but I was also wild. I was in and out of trouble, which kept me off a lot of the school teams. My main sport was baseball. I'm a natural athlete and can play any sport really well, but it wasn't enough to keep me out of trouble. I was expelled three days before graduation.

Just before my senior year Owen got transferred to San Diego. My mom, Richard, and my sister Terry, who is by Owen and my mother, went with him while I stayed behind to finish school. When I got kicked out of school I went to San Diego, and on Jan. 3, 1963, I joined the Marine Corps. I picked up the nickname Red Dog while I was in Vietnam, which was ironic because Duane's nickname was Skydog.

There and Back

I AM A DECORATED Vietnam veteran and was given a medical discharge in March of 1967 for wounds I received fighting the Vietcong. My parents had moved to Jacksonville while I was in Vietnam, so that's where I shipped to when I received my discharge. I returned with my arm in a cast after being shot up pretty bad. I got hit in the left wrist, and the bullet came out my left forearm leaving a nice big hole. So, you can imagine being shot up, coming back home, and finding yourself lonely. You get a little, you touch the rose, and of course it's the best in the world. The first thing that lays a little on you and your history. Then bang — you're married! I married Sue. The first girl I met that paid any attention to me, and not long after that, she had a baby girl.

I started working for Western Electric, but I couldn't use my left hand very well after being shot up. I heard they were going to fire me because I wasn't fast enough. So instead of waiting for them to fire me I quit. Knowing what I know now sure was a stupid move on my part, I'm talking lawsuit big time! Anyway, I came home one day to nothing but one fork in the silverware drawer. Sue was gone, I got divorced, lost my job, and life seemed like the pits. Us coming home from Vietnam, being called killers, murderers and every other thing imaginable, and now this. Nice lick huh?

Now I'm selling shoes at Montgomery Wards when my ex-mother-in-law starts playing games and not letting me see my daughter. You know shit like: "You can see her. No you can't. Yes you can." Then they'd be gone when I got there. One night I had a pretty good buzz and decided to go over, but they said, no, that I couldn't see her. Well, I kicked the doorframe in — it only took one kick — and the door opened. I was more surprised and shocked than anyone. I walked in and watched her sleeping for a minute or two and then split.

Of course they took out a warrant for my arrest. Wouldn't you know it? Here it goes again!

That was kind of funny in its own right. I'm in Montgomery Wards, helping a lady try on shoes and look up to see two plainclothes cops right there in the store. Well, they handcuffed and arrested me, and there I went, led from one end of the store to the other with my hands cuffed behind my back. I see the store full of people watching and staring. I could hear them saying under their breath, and out loud, "Oh no! I wonder what he's done?" So off to jail I went, locked up for thirty days. Luckily my friend's dad and his uncle, who was like my own uncle, helped me out. They paid a little money under the table, and after 18 to 21 days I shipped out on a freighter through the Panama Canal — right back to Vietnam as a Merchant Marine.

The first trip back to Nam really started to open my eyes and bring about some changes. I saw war differently. I was letting my hair grow out and becoming a hippie. I started to think war was a scam. Now I realize that when I was a Marine I was brainwashed like all the other marines — for freedom. Shit! I was starting to think it was more like fighting to put money into somebody's pocket: Uncle Sam's pocket. All of our soldiers that got killed, all the people that got killed on both sides, for what? For some assholes to get rich? You know, don't get me wrong, I'd be the first one to fight if someone were to strike our country. I'll always be a Marine until the day I die. I mean if somebody came over knocking on our back door, you better get out there and fight. Fight for our country. That's the way I was in Nam. If you got a wild hair to run and they didn't shoot you, I would have shot your ass. Sorry, I know that sounds mean, but think about it. If you ran, five or six guys might stand the chance of being killed because you took off and left a hole in the line. So fuck it! You run, you die.

In reality war sucked! I mean it sucked big time! Those were the sentiments I was adopting. I remember reading in the newspaper Stars & Stripes, the U.S. Armed Forces newspaper, that all the hippies were against us. I remember when we came home people used to shout "Killer! Murderer!" and it made you feel like shit. Do you know what it's like to come home from war thinking you've done the right thing, except everyone thinks you're a dick for standing up for your country? I had enough. I was shot up in Nam, then dumped on when I got home. My way to cope was to take another pain pill and drink a few beers. No problem no more.

While I was in the war, I thought I was doing the right thing by fighting for freedom. And believe me, if you were Charlie I'd cut your throat in a minute. I'd pump more rounds in your ass than Carter has farter starters. You're not going to get up and kill me. War does things to you like that. Things you don't know about until years later, even if then. You know, it gets locked so deep somewhere in your brain just waiting to get out, so you wake up at night with Charlie on your back and you're fighting for your life. Your wife is scared to death and doesn't move or blink an eye for a few seconds until she's sure you've got your thoughts back together. Then you realize you just had one hell of a dream. It must be like hell for her too, because she lives with the thought that you might wake up and think she's Charlie and go after her. That must be a nice feeling to live with huh? So, you see war even effected people that didn't go. I don't hold any grudge against people that burned their draft cards or ran to Canada. That's what we were supposedly fighting for — Freedom. And in my book, that means if you don't want to fight you shouldn't have to.

To make a long story short, on our way through the Panama Canal, I picked up two A&P shopping bags full of weed. Panama Red, kick-ass reefer. The best and probably still the best. I brought that, and some Vietnam Green back home with me. Don't you all just love these names? It makes it sound heavy doesn't it?

At home I was selling nickel bags on the street, so I had that going for me. I worked at the newsstand next to a go-go bar. Go-go bars, you remember that shit? The girls would wear a two-piece and waggle their stuff right in front of you. You were supposed to get all excited and say, "Oh, here's my dollar," and lay a few bills on 'em. Bull shit! It was nothing for me to get to know those girls. I worked next door, and they'd come in all the time. We had a section for porno books and magazines, all kinds of nasty stuff, and I could kind of just ease up to girls and pop off their rose. There were some girls though, no way. The only thing they'd do is straight up dance for tips. But, the few I had the pleasure of meeting and setting up a very nice business relationship with, they were all right. We took care of each other 50-50, and things went great for a while.

Around about the same time, I wanted to enter college to be a lawyer. First, I figured I needed to develop some pretty good study habits. I decided a couple years of junior college wouldn't hurt then I could go on to law school, so I enrolled in Florida Junior College at Jacksonville. Well, the first semester I'm doing great. I'm getting As and Bs, but I'm also doing eight bottles of Robitussin AC a day, that's Robitussin with Codeine — AC: "and Codeine."

I had sixteen drugstores set up on the lam because you could only get Robitussin AC with a signature. They'd also only give you one bottle in a 24-hour period. Everyday I could hit my eight drug stores, grab eight bottles, and still have a back up for eight more the next day. I'd also run up a few Dexamils, which are diet pills, just to stay awake. Man my guts must have looked like paste and glue. I stayed on the nod, and I wore dark shades. I'd nod, snap back and stay right on track, but somehow I managed to turn in my assignments. I could stand up between nods and speak out in class, and the instructors liked that. Hell, they couldn't see I was on the nod. I put my book up like I was reading. With the dark shades on they couldn't tell.

Calling of the Brotherhood

It was 1969 when I met Duane Allman. Actually, I had heard him, but I didn't know who he was back then. It was like the Pied Piper calling, and I mean that. I know all this mysticism might sound crazy, but you'll understand later. It was like being called by the big spirit in the sky. Like the calling of the disciples.

During school I used to go down to the gie dunk, a Marine Corp., term for a snack bar. I could get candy, Cokes, milk, hamburgers and play the jukebox. Well, I heard this song, "The Weight" by Aretha Franklin. I wasn't sure what it was, but man it struck a nerve. It had this killer slide guitar intro. Now I didn't know slide from picking or jumping up and down. To me, up until then, music just kind of took up space. I used to dance a little, and I used to follow the beat, but that was about it for dancing. I just fell in love with that guitar. Not that I didn't like the whole song, I did, but the intro just grabbed me like nothing else and it wouldn't let go. Every time I went to the gie dunk I played that song "The Weight" by Aretha Franklin.

One day I was there and a friend of my ex-brother-in-law, Dennis Blake, walked up and said Duane Allman and Johnny Johanson (Jaimoe) were playing at a love-in, the parties with music, hippies, drink and all kinds of assorted characters, on Sunday down at the Forrest Inn.

Well, you know me, I came up with some crazy comment like: "Who in the hell is Duane Allman and Johnny Johanson?"

My man Dennis says to me, "Man you don't know? You play those damn records there on every day."

I said: "What records?" I didn't have a clue what he was talking about. I didn't know the name of the songs, but I damn sure knew the numbers on the jukebox. So Dennis walked over and played it. He told me about Duane, who he was playing with, (Aretha Franklin). He also told me about Jaimoe, and who he was playing with (Otis Redding). Hell, I didn't even know who they were, but I knew the songs, and I liked what I heard.

I said, "Shit! If this guy is going to play the Forrest Inn on Sunday, I'm going to be there." And of course, a love-in meant ladies, so I knew for sure I'd be there.

I showed up Sunday at the love-in and the band was set up outside. It was a gathering of hippies, an outdoor party held on the grassy area outside of the Forrest Inn. The building was off the road apiece, and the band was set up a ways back and faced the road. I was dressed a little different than normal, so I must have looked like a fish out of water compared to Duane and the guys. I dressed down a lot from the long hair thing because I didn't want to attract attention to my other activities; selling reefer and working with the ladies of the night. I still remember what I wore; a black hat with a rounded brim that I kept turned down in front and back so you could just barely see my eyes. I had on a black T-shirt, a Jungle Jim jacket, Levis, and brown moccasins. By this time my hair was down the back of my neck and just over my ears. I wasn't really a low life, but I have to say I probably left the impression of quite the low life. If certain people saw me dressed like that, they would surely think I had ulterior motives, or that I was in some way connected with drugs, and I was. I remember now I also had a beard and my first set of hippie beads — real sharp, little round wooden balls of various sizes, some big and some small. I think they may have actually belonged to a friend of mine Sharon, a really nice girl. A big titty girl, and she was about as sweet as she could be. About the sweetest rose I'd ever tasted. Well, that is except for a friend of mine from Louisville, but more on her a little later.

For me that day was the beginning of the calling of the Brotherhood. Man, hearing Duane play I couldn't believe my ears. Play like nothin' I'd ever heard before. He had some of the finest licks in the world. His guitar seemed to talk to you. Call out your name. They could all damn sure play, but most of all I remember him and Jaimoe. Maybe it's just that they stood out in my mind more than the others who were there with their own bands, like the Second Coming: Berry Oakley, Butch Trucks, Dickey Betts, Nasty Lord John, Reese Wynans (who later went on to play with Stevie Ray Vaughan), and the Rhino; Larry Reinhardt (who went on to play with Iron Butterfly).

I remember Jaimoe playing the drums. He used his elbow and hands, laying them down on the conga just to get that certain sound he wanted at that one specific time. I sure never knew music could sound like that. Like I said, to me it always just took up space and sounded like background music. This day ended that. This day was different. After listening to Duane, I thought to myself, man I have to meet this cat.

I wandered on in, and the next thing I knew Duane and I were talking. I'm telling him I never heard anything like that before. I explained I couldn't believe how I was hearing him, fine and pretty, rough and raunchy, all at once and all wrapped up together in one. I told him I could feel it in my whole body. I told him that before today, music just seemed to take up space. The next thing I knew he asked if I happened to have a joint. Well, shit, of course I did. That was right up my alley. I said, "Yeah I have a joint. I have a joint of fine Panama Red, kick-ass bud," and away we go to a little boiler room in the back.

There was just enough room for the two of us to sit on a couple of old crates to smoke a joint. We smoked, and shot the shit for a long time. I told him a little about being in Vietnam. How fucked up I thought the war was, what I thought it was all about, and everything I had to do. That's when my eyes really opened up.

Duane had this way of talking that made you instantly realize he didn't bullshit. Almost like he could look inside and see how messed up I was after the war. As I remember, we sat there for quite a long time. We smoked two joints, and got pretty fucked up. Towards the end, he just shook his head back and forth saying: "Man don't be a musician 'cause they are all messed up." He was excited though. He told me he was putting together a new band with Jaimoe, Butch, Berry and Dickey, and he was hoping like hell his little brother might leave California to come back home so he could start Beelzebub. That was the name he had in mind: Beelzebub. He said Gregg would come back, and man can he sing. He can sing the blues like nothing you've ever heard. He can sing like a canary. Like nobody else.

I didn't meet Jaimoe back then as Jaimoe. I met him as "Frown," who I mistakenly referred to as "Fran." I kept it all mixed up for a couple of days too. I kept calling him "Fran." I think I spoke with Fran first. I just walked up to him and told him I was Red Dog. Jaimoe looked at me and said, "I'm Frown." Now you know me, I thought he said Fran, so now the first Red Doggyism is born within the Allman Brothers Band. "Fran." There I go again. Mixing up and turning something sideways so it ends up a Doggyism.

Jaimoe and I hit it off right from the start. At least in my eyes we sure did. I know this isn't the reason, and forgive me if it even sounds like I'm saying it is. Our relationship is much deeper than that, but I did have an act. I could play and act like I was black. I could go through the hand and body motions, and if you heard my raps in a dark room, you know a room with a real low light, or even a blacklight, it almost looked like I was black. I think living most of my life in the Florida sun contributed to it. Plus the fact that I'm dark skinned for a red-headed person. I can go out in the sun and not burn like most redheads. Get a little sun one day and turn brown the next, and for a redhead that's pretty good.

I also played a lot of baseball with black kids. Being in the Marines, I picked up on styles quick. Hell, I can talk to anybody. I can do the street rap, bench rap, backroom rap, negotiating table rap. Whatever the situation calls for, I can go with it. Except for Tracy, she just blew my cool all to shit. I'll tell you a little bit more about that later.

Hell, I'll give you an example of someone not knowing if I was black or white. On my first trip back to Vietnam as a Merchant Marine, we stopped in Japan for 16 days to load and offload supplies. I was the mess-man on board, and my good buddy James Osbey was the baker. One night while we were on liberty leave from the ship, sweet daddy James and I decided to go out partying. We ended up at this club in Tokyo with real low light. A brother eased on up to sweet daddy and said, "Hey is this guy black or white," referring to me. I was doing my act. He said, "He looks white, but damn! He sure acts like a stone cold brother." So that's all I'm saying, and I don't mean anything by it. I just had the ability to get over no matter where I was.

Anyway, back to the love-in. You know, I don't remember seeing Mike Callahan there. He was one of the original roadies for the Allman Brothers Band. Mike is still one of my best friends in the whole world, but I do believe he was there; along with Big Linda, Berry's wife, and Butch's wife, Linda, who we used to call Momma Trucks. I also think Hop, and Pam, who was Rhino's wife, were there. Maybe even Judy Seymore and Mary, who I would shortly be sharing the Green House with. That's where the famous jams went down.

I know one thing now that I think about it. I told Frown I wanted to meet Duane, and he was the one that introduced us. Well, he didn't really introduce us. I think I may have mentioned that I'd like to meet him, and Frown said, "Well just go on over and introduce yourself, "so that's about what I did. Our conversations used to be a lot like rapping, Frown's and mine. They went something like:

"Where you from."

"Nice playing."

"I like your style."

They were short raps. I don't know how to tell you, but we really seemed to connect. At least to me we did. I'll say this, the calling of the brotherhood was definitely at hand, and I was a changed man. I heard the calling of the disciples.

Dedication

On Monday morning I was on top of the world. I'd heard some kick-ass music, and felt like I connected with Jaimoe, Duane and some special people. About the only bad thing was that I was a little sore from going at it all night long with my hot momma, but I kicked it in. I did my first bottle of AC for the day and headed straight for the gie dunk right off the bat. I played "The Weight" first thing. I mean I walked in and straight to the jukebox. Bingo! I dropped in my coin, and Duane was playing.

School went by all right for a Monday. I stayed on the nod most of the day and nothing much really happened. I did manage to drop out of my SDS club (Students for a More Democratic Society). It was supposed to be a club on improving America, maybe something similar to being in the Young Republicans. Real good club here. Yeah right! I'd been back from Vietnam for about two years, and they started saying shit against the country. Talking about communism. Not just saying any little thing here or there. Man, I could have gone through those people like water. Naive, just a little. Boy, I was out of there. At least I did one good thing the day after I met Duane. I dropped that club like a bad habit.

Anyway, things went slow there for a while. Two weeks or so went by until I found out Big Bro, that's Duane, was going to jam again. One of the girls at a bar I hung out in told me he was going to play at the Comic Book Club. I think on a Thursday night. They (the girls at the bar) were into long hair and music, and knew everything that was going on.

That was my first encounter with the "groupie grapevine," the fastest telegraph in the universe. It was also the first time I ever remember seeing Joe Dan. I waited around all night until about three o'clock in the morning to hear Duane play again. In the meantime, I had business to attend to so it wasn't really that bad of a wait. I had a few small deals to get rid of my reefer and needed to check on my girls. You know, make sure they were okay.

When I worked at the newsstand, I had this little side business set up. I would take orders for nickel bags during work. The little brown envelope about an inch-and-a-half wide and two inches long, filled with the equivalent of a matchbox of reefer. The way it worked was, I would take the orders, tell them what time to meet me and what corner to be on, they would give me five dollars for the bag, and I took the reefer later. I never blew it either. I used to keep more times and more street corners in my head than you can imagine.

I also had two partners who helped me out. Two black guys: Jerome and Notta. Jerome was an ex-Marine with two young kids and worked as an accountant. I met him in a bar one night and we just hit it off. We became good friends, and after a while, we were in business. He had a contact for boy, that's heroin, and reefer. I had the reefer and girls, so we put it all together and ran one bus. We eventually dropped the boy.

In the course of putting my little business together, along came Notta. A friend of Jerome's who was just the opposite of Jerome. Notta talked shit all the time. Bouncing the bounce and walking the walk. He wore these glasses and was real hyper, except when he was on the nod. Man, I loved those two guys. They were real close to me. We could sell more on the street than you could shake a stick at. We could do it right in front of pedestrians or the police without them even knowing.

While I took orders at the newsstand and collected my money, my two partners were doing the same thing. Later I would go meet my first customer at the exact time and place we set up. I would take the nickel bag in my hand so when we spotted each other, all we did was say, "what's happening?" and slap hands as we passed. I passed the reefer during the hand slap. It was a damn slick move if I do say so myself. It just looked like two guys walking down the street saying hey. But, if they didn't show up, I wouldn't stick around and wait. Goodbye. I had another corner to get to.
So remember all good things must come to an end.

I took care of business and headed on over to the Comic Book Club, a rough and tough bottle club. It was about 1:30 in the morning by the time I got there, and I think there were only twenty people in the club. It looked like they were all there to see Duane. When I walked in, the band that was playing included Ronnie Van Zant, Gary Rossington, and Allen Collins, the basis of what later became Lynyrd Skynyrd. I think they went by the name of One Percent. Anyway, I sat down for a while, and it wasn't too long until Duane, Joe Dan, and Dickey came in. They sat down with a girl named Trudy, and after a while, they got up to jam.

My good brother Joe Dan had a tiny dark mustache, wore a white cowboy hat and played bass. Dickey also wore a white cowboy hat, and Duane had on a green Stetson. Thing was, they only played a couple of songs. I don't think the club owner wanted them to go off into any long jams, so he only allowed them a very short time. But, even in that short time, they blew me away. The Pied Piper reached out and touched me again. I mean I'm really getting sucked in now.

Afterwards at just about the time everybody was leaving, I was headed out the door when Duane saw me and said, "Hey man what's happening?"

Then a little louder than I would have liked, he said, "Hey you got any speed?"

I mean to me it sounded like a damn foghorn going off. In reality, it probably wasn't that loud, but I damn sure thought it was. There I was standing by the door holding a few bags of reefer just about to go into orbit because of how loud I thought he said it.

I said, "No, man. I'm sorry," and said it real soft and quiet like as I kind of looked around to make sure no one heard us. Then we went on out to the parking lot.

I remember I had an old Chevy Impala and Duane drove a beat up old Ford that we used to call the "Blues Mobile." That's what it looked like, a beat up old blues mobile. Duane and I were parked just a couple cars apart from each other, and I watched him put his and Dickey's guitars, and Joe Dan's bass into the trunk. When no one else was around except them, I walked on over and said, "I ain't got no speed, but I do have some reef."

He said, "Hell yeah!" So I gave him a nickel bag of red.

I told him, "That's all right man. No charge."

He said, "Thanks man. That was nice of you."

And I said, "Man, it was worth it just to hear you play," and that was about all. We parted and drove off, and I don't think either of us knew at the time his band was about to grow.

I was a dedicated person though, and I think Duane knew this from the talk we had in the boiler room a couple weeks earlier. Mainly from me telling him about the war, and how you had to stick together, even in the worst part of battle. When it looks like it's all over and you're going down for the count, if you stick together and everyone does their job, you can turn the thing around and win. I do believe in sticking together. I'm a diehard because I'll stick it out until the end. I mean I'll go through hell to try and make something work.

Anyway, things continued as normal until one afternoon when I was working at the newsstand and this girl Dottie came in. I noticed her when she came in, but I didn't really pay any attention to her. Not enough to think she did anything, at least I didn't think so, until there was no one in the store and she came up and whispered to me, "Do you smoke pot?"

To my surprise, I said, "Yes!" I mean I was really cool about not selling to people I didn't know or that didn't come with good recommendations.

Then she asked, "Do you know where to get some?" There I went again saying yes to somebody when maybe I shouldn't have. There was something about her though. Even with no customers in the store, she was nervous and talking softly, so I just figured everything was all right. Somehow, I could always sense from people if they were honest or not. Vibes is what we used to say, the vibes. You know how people can sometimes feel things coming off other people like good or bad vibes? I became more and more aware of this ability to read people with each passing day of my life. Anyway, I went ahead and made a deal. I got Dottie's address, told her I'd meet her at her place after it got dark, and I headed on over about nine o'clock.

When I got there, she invited me in. Now this is exactly what I was hoping for from the beginning. In the back of my mind I was thinking, "Hey I got a shot," I wasn't only thinking about selling reefer. After all, being the stud I thought I was, I was good and ready to go in like she asked. But, I started hearing voices from inside the house. No way! I wasn't going to go into her apartment just to sell reefer when there were other people inside.

I said, "No, thanks. There's other people in there, and I don't sell in front of other people."

Even though she said it was okay, that they were her friends, I told her, "No, thanks. I'll do it right here."

She still tried to get me to come in a couple times, but I didn't. So she went back, got a few bucks, and came out with the money. I sold her two nickel bags like we talked about at the newsstand, then I split.

It wasn't until a little later when I learned who the other people inside were — Duane, Berry, Butch, Big Linda, Hop, and a few others. They were actually waiting for me. Duane had asked Dottie to come by the newsstand and see me.

Rendezvous in Time

THE NEXT TIME I heard Duane play was at the Jacksonville Beach Coliseum. The Second Coming and the Load would occasionally play there on weekends. That was about the time the hippie scene was starting to hit Jacksonville. There weren't that many clubs where freestyle bands could play. I remember one other place that was pretty hip; a little blacklight club off of Roosevelt Highway called the Scene.

Anyway, during breaks at the coliseum Duane and I used to ride around and smoke. That's when we really got to know each other. Sometimes Berry or Frown would ride around with us, and I would have a bottle or two of AC that we drank. Of course that's how Frown got his nickname, from nodding off all the time and frowning. It's like when someone nods off, they frown. And Frown would frown. Those were some good times. Now things were looking better, and I was beginning to have fun again. The war was starting to fade into the back of my mind.

That was when Duane told me he was going to name the band Beelzebub. The first time I ever remember seeing the original Allman Brothers lineup play together was when they played a few songs as Beelzebub. They played during a Second Coming gig at the Jacksonville Armory. Gregg had shown up, and the beginning of a great band was born. They played their asses off with hardly any rehearsal. It was just like Big Bro told me, "Brother Gregg can sing the blues, and man, you can just feel it down in your soul." Man he was right too.

Around about this time, I was hanging out a lot with Duane and Frown. Now that Gregg was there, we were starting to become running partners. We started hanging together and making runs to the "syrup house." A drugstore down in Jacksonville I had lined up. The druggist Doc Campbell and I had the same last names. Back in those days it was legal to buy Robitussin AC over the counter, but you had to sign for it. You also had to wait two days until you could buy it again. Like I said earlier, I had 16 drug stores I could buy from, but none were like Doc's. He knew what I was there for and didn't seem to care. He would see us coming in the door and start mixing syrup. He was an old fellow already, and well remembered now by Kim Payne, Gregg, Frown, and myself. Anyway, after we got the syrup, we'd buy a couple jawbreaker-sized pieces of orange bubble gum, and a strawberry milkshake to kill the taste of the AC. Damn it was nasty!

About the same time all this was happening, I moved into the Green House on Riverside Drive. When I moved in, there was already a girl named Mary living there along with Judy, who later married Ronnie Van Zant, and Dean, who went on to be the assistant road manager for Lynyrd Skynyrd. He later died in the plane crash.

I remember Judy was sometimes doing a thing with Gregg. Baby Face, that's Gregg, could just walk in a room and it was like somebody watered the rose garden. Long blond hair, played the organ, and signing the blues like he did. It sounded like a black man singing. Shit, he could write his own ticket. He still can today. It's a natural born fact.

The beginning was here. Duane had put his band together along with the road crew.

Twiggs was the first person to be hired. Even before B.O. (Berry Oakley) and Jaimoe. He was born in Macon and basically lived there his whole life. Twiggs was the first road manager of the band, but Willie Perkins was always on the horizon. He would become the band's second road manager after Twiggs offed the guy in Buffalo for not paying us the money for a gig. I would say Brother Twiggs was a perfectionist. Even that might be selling him short. If there is a higher level than a perfectionist that's where he would be. I'll go into more detail about Twiggs the mmmullettttt (Mullett) later.

Joe Dan Petty, who had played bass in a band Dickey and Dale had before the Second Coming, was offered a job as a roadie, but Joe Dan couldn't leave home because there was no money to be made. He was already working days and playing clubs in Orlando to support his wife and two kids (Jody and J.J.). If he had left right then, they would have starved.

I don't exactly know when I met Mike, that's Mike "The Mander" Callahan. He was a character too. He and Berry were friends and used to work together when Berry played with the Romans. Mike was the soundman, and that's back when the soundman did the monitors and mixed the house sound. I remember rapping with Mike, and it seemed like each of us were just there at the same time.

The Mander could talk numbers like you wouldn't believe. He knew the damn number of everything. Sometimes I think he just made up numbers to cover something that was wrong. Just so you wouldn't know he really fucked up. Don't get me wrong, Mander was good. I've seen him make things work when they shouldn't have. That probably came from working at the zoo and on the shrimp boats while he grew up in Tarpon Springs. Okay, it may have also come from working with bands that didn't have any money. Learning that you didn't have any choice but to make it work. Which was something I was also soon to learn.

As I think about it, we may have met at one of the jams or at the Grey House where B.O., Dickey, the Rhino, and Hop lived. It was across Riverside Drive and three houses down from the Green House. I remember Berry lived down the stairs on the left, and Rhino lived in the apartment right across the hall from him. Dickey lived above Berry in the apartment upstairs, and Hop, who was an acquaintance of Donna's, lived across from Dickey. Hop was a friend of Donna's, and Donna and Duane used to stay with Hop a lot of the time. Hop had the best apartment of all, with a nice big room on the back and windows all around on three sides.

There was also Kim Payne, my man Payne's Ass or Slim Jenkins. He came from Montgomery, Alabama, and his dad was the captain of the state police. Slim was, and is a great person who will be my brother forever. He took care of the guitars and amps. He was a workhorse too. I mean a workhorse! Not that Mike and myself weren't. Hell, we all had to be, but Kim really was. I remember he had just gotten out of the Navy and was doing a little roadie work in L.A. when Gregg lived out there. That's how Gregg and Kim hooked up and got to know each other.

When Gregg left L.A. to head back to Jacksonville, he told Kim if things worked out he'd try to get him a job as a roadie. Kim didn't think anything of it. He thought he was just bullshittin' like, "Yeah, man. I'm not going to hear from you. You probably won't call."

Well sure enough, Maximus, that's Gregg, called Kim and said come on. So Payne's Ass headed to Jacksonville. He jumped on his trusty big bad bike, a little 350cc Honda, and he rode that little bitch all the way across the country! All the way to Jacksonville with what little money he had, and a few clothes stuffed into a saddlebag.

If you ever see a picture of Twiggs, and you can see his right arm, you'll see a tattoo with the names of the original ten members of the Allman Brothers Band in the order that they joined. The tattoo wraps around his arm and starts out with Duane in the middle. Next to it reading left to right is Twiggs, followed by Berry, Jaimoe, Gregg, Dickey, Butch, Mike, Kim, and Red Dog. This is also shown on the inner sleeve of the Duane Allman Anthology album cover. Twiggs had the brothers sit in the canoe in the order that they came into the band.

Now the band is all together and we are starting to rock.

It was the Calling of the Brotherhood — an unseen force leading us to a rendezvous in time.

A Little Earlier

Twiggs worked for Brother Phil Walden, who was the manager of Otis Redding up in Macon, Georgia. Phil sent him out as the road manager with various soul acts where he spent some time with Little Richard, and received one hell of an education on how to take care of business on the road.

Phil was asked by Atlantic Records to get in touch with Brother Duane, so he sent Twiggs to Muscle Shoals, Alabama to check him out. They met and Twiggs listened to Duane do some session work. Then Twiggs went back and told Phil, "The white boy can play his ass off. He's the best white boy I ever heard play the blues."

Phil had been booking soul bands for years, and Jaimoe played with a lot of them; Otis Redding, Percy Sledge, and Clarence Carter to name a few. Phil told Duane nobody knew how good Jaimoe was, "He either plays over everybody's head, or he ain't worth a shit. He plays all this stuff that nobody understands."

Jaimoe hooked up with Duane at Muscle Shoals when Phil asked Duane to listen to him. Duane had a place out side of town in the country, so when Jaimoe got there he stayed with Duane, but they never said much to each other, just played, and that's how they communicated. All that stuff that Jaimoe was playing was evidently over a lot of people's heads, but it was right up Duane's alley. After Duane and Jaimoe met, they played together for about six weeks until Duane had enough of studio work. Then they split and went to Jacksonville to scoop Berry.

Now, Duane told me Phil said to him he wanted to be his manager, and Duane told Phil he wanted to put a band together. Phil said, "Fine," and Duane said, "You got a hundred thousand dollars?"

Phil said "Yes," so Duane said, "Then you're my manager."

They shook hands and that was that.

Trippin' to Macon

AROUND THE END OF March in 1969, Dickey had a run-in with the law. The police came to his apartment and he threw some pot that was lying on the coffee table out the window. When he threw the pot out the window it just went with the wind. The police didn't arrest him, but they were hip to him. The next day the band packed up and headed for Macon, leaving the old ladies at home. So you can see right off the bat, the band is on the run.

I had to stay and complete my semester in junior college because I wanted to finish what I started. One day Judy wanted to go see Gregg in Macon, so she dosed Dean and me and drug us with her. That was my first trip to Macon and also my first trip on acid. I didn't get off too good on the stuff Judy gave me, but when we got there Gregg walked up and put a hit of Psilocybin, that's a pill from of the mushroom, in my mouth. The mushroom took me to the cosmos. I saw the world like I never saw it before. If you have ever tripped then you know what I'm talking about. Can I get an A-men?

The first few times I tripped I would think a lot about the war. One time we were sitting around the apartment at 309 College Street listening to music with the trip light going, which is a vibration light that blinked with sound. We also had an old fashion Coke machine that you had to push the handle down on to get a drink. It had four selections, Pabst, Bud, Schlitz, and Coca-Cola. It took a quarter, but Twiggs always had to open it up — no money. The wall by the entrance door was painted different colors in a big square with the outer square black. The next one in was white, then red, then green, then white, and this went down to a little square in the middle. It looked real neat with the trip light going.

Well, this time I was thinking out loud about the war and said, "They're everywhere! They're all around us!" until Duane said, "Shut up Red Dog." So I went on tripping with no more thoughts on that. He was a strong person and his words meant a lot to me. You might say he led me across the water.

You have to trip four or five times to get where you are still in control. Just some minor adjustments you have to put together, and then you can take your trip where you want to go, not where it wants to take you.

I missed the first road trip to Boston. The band played at the Boston Tea Party, which was owned by Don Law, who would become a good friend and promoter, and still is. The band had to stay in a condemned apartment building, and the J. Geils Band was staying across the hall. Neither band had any money at the time, and the living conditions were not what you would want to write home about, if you know what I mean. The bums even threw a cherry bomb in the rooms because they wanted them out.

But, talk about good timing, the same day the band got back to Macon, Gregg left for Daytona Beach. I had gotten permission to take my exams early, and I finished the same day, so on the way he stopped by the Green House in Jacksonville and picked me up. Away we went.

We were off on a trip that has lasted 32 years.

The Brotherhood & Beelzebub Curse

BEELZEBUB — THE DEVIL'S RIGHT-HAND man. For about a week or two that's what Duane called the band, until he changed his mind and called it the Allman Brothers Band. In hindsight, I think it was probably a good decision. Maybe a great decision. I think changing the name was very, very hip. Look at the name Allman, All-Man, in biblical days meaning everybody. And this was the way Big Bro looked at it. One for all and all for one: No separation. So maybe for this we are soon to be awarded good things, like trips to the graveyard, and our one-room apartment on College Street in Macon.

The main reason he didn't want to change the name was because Duane and Gregg were better known than everyone else. Duane didn't want separation from him and the rest of the Band. He got mad when the first album The Allman Brothers Band came out. Yes, I would say Duane was upset. If you open up the album there's a picture on the far right of them standing side by side. He told me he thought that separated him and Gregg from everybody else, and the band was not him and Gregg, but six musicians and four roadies. He didn't like it, but it was too late to change, so it stayed that way.

The six musicians and four roadie thing also carried on when Phil would call a band meeting. When he called a meeting Duane would take the whole band, that's the six musicians and four roadies. Phil would say, "Do I have to meet with the roadies too?" He would much rather it just be him and Duane, not even the other musicians much less the roadies, but Duane said, "You called a band meeting, and this is the band."

To Phil (Mister Clean), this wasn't fun and games but business with a little humor. Duane was the Preacher and Berry was the Deacon. Big Bro spoke some, but not much, that was left up to Berry. He did most of the rapping, and I can't remember Duane ever going against anything Berry said, at least not at a meeting. He would just add the final exclamation mark meaning that whatever Berry said was the way it would be. You have to understand that Berry was smart. He also did the rapping between songs at the gigs. The Deacon.

Like I said, Beelzebub was the devil's right-hand man, and it makes you wonder. Looking back over the years, there seemed to be this cloud over us. Everything that happened just made us stronger and stronger until this day, when the chips are down and dirty, and we're at the bottom of one of those friggin' traps. But, the Brotherhood will pull together, tighter and tighter each time.

The music is great, and it's the main thing that has kept this band going. To me the Allman Brothers make the best music. It's the main driving force. They play from the heart and soul. They play with the spirits. This music is not played anywhere else on Earth. Even now, Jaimoe, Dickey, Gregg, and Butch can go off and play in other bands, solo or whatever, and each one has had great bands, but it's nothing like the Allman Brothers.

Duane went off and played with Delaney and Bonnie and Eric Clapton a couple of times, but he couldn't wait to get back home. He would tell me they played good, but not like us. Like brother Duane told me the night before he departed this dimension, "This is a religion we are spreading. The music will always bring us back." Think about that. He went to get people into our church so they would become one of us. Mushroom people, that's what I've always called Allman Brothers music lovers.

I think when you trip together a lot it makes you tight also. Especially when your ass ain't got no money and there has to be four or five of you to go somewhere. The first days in Macon were like that. The whites and blacks wanted to get us because nobody in Macon had long hair. There used to be a solid line of cars; bumper to bumper in both directions all day on Sundays just to see the hippies. And this went on all week, but Sunday was the worst.

You see we didn't have money or gigs. I gave the band my disability checks of $100 each month, which I got for being wounded in Vietnam (U.S.M.C.), and that helped. But we really only had each other and the great music to get us through, so we hung together.

One night we were all up on Coleman Hill in Macon, tripping. We were down on the right side of the hill where there were three or four oak trees surrounded by some hedges. The trees had all grown together at the top, and you could lay under them and not be seen from the road. This was a couple of days after Gregg and Kim went off and left me in Gainesville, Florida, after we had been there a couple days partying. Anyway, Duane was lying next to me, and while we were lying under the trees with the wind blowing really hard, he said, "You are thinking about leaving."

I said, "How did you know?"

He said, "I can tell. You're my brother, and I know. It's only been a short time, but I know you."

Then he said, "Look up at the trees, see how they grow together. No matter how hard the wind blows they don't separate."

I think that says it all, and I've lived with that statement for 32 years. We were tighter than a gnat's ass stretched over a rain barrel, and the mushrooms really helped a lot. A band that eats, sleeps, drinks, and gets a little rose together is going to get tight. And we definitely got tight. The mushroom is a great symbol of that. If you take a picture of the Allman Brothers mushroom and turn it sideways you can see the nasty root going into that sweet rose.

Yes, we liked ladies. We were nine gorillas and one coyote; Gregg was the coyote. The nine of us would take your lady from you like Sam and Dave said in their song, we will gorilla your old lady. But Gregg, all he had to do was walk in a room and the roses would get wet. I mean the coyote could make the rose talk. Oh Lord, don't let Baby Face get up on the B-3 and start singing. Shit! Tighten up the attic momma, here they come.

Brother Duane was no slouch either. I was standing right beside him one time when this chick told him that she came all over herself during one of his solos. My man smiled and we moved on. You see there are some bad dudes here all the way around.

Jaimoe, he was snakey. He'd come and get your chick, whoever it might be that night, while you were sleeping and take her in the bathroom. You'd wake up the next morning saying how did the rose open up? It was closed last night.

Of course, there was the same problem with Betts and Trucks. You see there were ten of us, but we could only afford two rooms. When one of us got lucky, everybody got lucky, or at least got to watch. One for all and all for one. The Brotherhood.

The Brotherhood, we weren't just cocky, we were cock hard. Even the sophisticated one, Butch. He didn't half-step. When he came off the woodwork — he came off the woodwork! It was great. He seemed to always pull a fox, and we used to just stand back and watch. Trucksey was so cool. Once he would slip the old johnson to them, you couldn't pull the chick away with a come-along. Except you had to watch out for the Coyote, all watching out for the Coyote.

Then of course Betts would come along and do his thing; like the first orgy we had. We just got the second apartment at 309 College Street, and the chicks that lived across the hall would come over. We met a young couple, and couple of girls from Wesleyan, which was an all-girls college on the edge of town. I think Kim, Mike, Gregg, myself, Jaimoe, Twiggs, the photographer who took the pictures for our first album; Stephen Paley, and of course our guests, were in our new apartment. We had taken some Psilocybin, and were sitting on the floor in a big circle smoking because we didn't have furniture; just mattresses and a cheap stereo system. We were sitting around getting high when my man Betts and this girl Patty stand up and get naked. I mean they just took their clothes off right there. Kim and Debbie followed right behind, and it started. I think the young couple was really freaked, but my point being that when Brother Dickey wants to throw it around, he throws it around. He could gangbuster the rose in a New York second.

Now the roadies didn't bring up the rear by no means, we had our harem. Like the time Mike Callahan and myself tripped in my apartment on Orange Terrace with two ladies from Atlanta; foxes I might add. We were upstairs in the loft at the foot of two double beds. I put three drops of liquid acid in each of the ladies mouths, and three in Mike's. As I was pulling the bottle away, an extra drop fell into Mike's mouth, so he starts saying I gave him four drops. He says this a couple times as I'm putting the bottle up above my mouth. Then he reached over to help me. He squeezed the bottle and a stream of acid went straight down my throat. Need I say more? Bye, bye, Red Dog. Acid trip #459. See you when you get back. There were about four hours or so that I can't tell you about, and never will be able to. We're talking blank. Hell, maybe Mike doesn't know what happened either. All I know is we were laying pipe the next morning, just like we started the night before.

Two-Lane Traffic

I'LL GIVE YOU AN idea of how much pipe we laid around the country. This promoter friend of ours, Larry Vaughan, from up around Chicago, was down South booking dates with Mr. Tony Rafeno. He told us that no matter where they went, every girl he met had been with somebody in the band. Hell, my step-dad Owen Coile even called our Winnebago a "whorehouse on wheels." Yes, back then, we thought our shit didn't stink, and it surely didn't. Play music, get high, get laid, that's all we had time for; except to get in a little minor trouble now and then.

Like the time leaving Memphis when Mike, this black chick and me were in the equipment truck on some two-lane highway. Once again we were out in the middle of nowhere, but this time we are not tripping. I was hung over real bad from the night before when we were at the amphitheater at the Memphis Zoo. I was doing some coke, and I got a really bad headache. I mean my head felt like someone took an axe and split it open. Worst headache I ever had. During the out, this girl starts taking care of me. Her name is Chris, but I'm not sure of her last name. She was washing my face and rubbing my neck with a cold wet rag, and she helped me get to the hotel and gave me a placidyl to go to sleep. These are strong for me and it knocked me on my butt. I remember Chris was leaving the room and I jumped out of bed when she was at the door. I was thinking I should be doing Red Dog things, but the second my feet hit the floor my head went into a spin, so I said goodbye and thanks. I got right back in bed, and went out like a light.

The next morning everyone left except Mike, the black chick, who we won't say was fat — just big boned, and me. Well, we were about to walk out the door when there was Chris. She came to say goodbye, and give me a picture she drew after she got home the night before. She gave me the picture, we said goodbye, and I haven't seen her since.

The picture was about five inches by six inches of a red Irish Setter, which actually looked a little like me. I can't say it was for sure an Irish Setter, maybe more of a mixed breed, with really long hairy ears, but that was my favorite. She signed the picture "love by the tail," and that's how I came up with the nickname for her of Chris "Love."

Anyway, we left the hotel and about two hours later we made a wrong turn. Well, I was driving and decided we needed to turn around, so there was this place; a nice place for that time period, a service area out in what I call the barelands. You know the places where there's nothing else around? You don't see a house or anything for miles. Then I made, or should I say, tried to make a U-turn just past the parking lot of the service area. I couldn't pull in the parking lot and turn around. No, that would have been too easy.

Well, I'm half way through my U-turn when the back wheel of the truck dropped off the road, and naturally it made the whole truck drop down. When the truck drops down, the trailer hitch and the trailer digs into the asphalt; deep down, about three inches. Now we can't go forward or backwards. We were stuck in the middle of the road in this great big "C" curve and traffic slowly started to back up in both directions. So we are out of the truck surveying the situation.

Now, this was a two-lane road, and we've got her blocked up for miles. I mean miles and miles. All these rednecks are walking up and looking at us, then at the truck. They even offered a couple suggestions, but they were looking at us really hard. Everyone was talking to us as our black friend gets out of the truck, and starts telling us what we should do. Now Mike and me are about to shit. Here we are in the backwoods of Mississippi, we got the road blocked, and these guys see we have a black chick with us who is running her mouth. Now in my mind she has just developed a bad case of dumb bitch syndrome. So I get a hold of her, and off to the truck we go doing a fast two-step shuffle. I'm telling her, "This is Missi-fuckin'-ssippi! Keep your ass in the truck and your friggin' big mouth shut." I sure as hell didn't want to buy the dirt in the backwoods of Mississippi.

While I was doing all this with the black chick, Mike was telling everyone, "We just picked her up hitchhiking." That's good ol' Mike, thinking fast. After a while a tow truck comes up. From where I do not know, but he gets us out in the nick of time. He more than likely saved our butts, because people were pissed and making comments like, "Stupid hippie nigger-lovin' motherfuckers," when at the same time we see the police coming behind us. Now we start thinking drugs and where are they?

Well, with a little good luck and fast moving we got free. Like I said, the police came from behind us, and the cars were every where; on the road, off the road, hell, they were everywhere. Which made it hard for the police to get to us. You see, they could see us, but couldn't get to us. So away we went, smokin' a reef and listening to our New York friend. Know what I mean? Good thing she was uppen the rose.

The Ghost of Dickey

NOW HERE'S SOMETHING ON an up note. It's one of my favorite tails, and I hope I can put it into words so you can see in your mind what I'm saying.

Brother Dickey is into Zen and meditates still to this day. Maybe about three or four months after we moved to Macon he was in the graveyard at Rosehill Cemetery. The graveyard is right next to the river, so in the mornings you get this low fog, like on this particular morning. It was just after sunrise and there was a low hanging fog over the graves.

Now the fog that I'm talking about, if you can visualize it, is a fog like in the Jack the Ripper movies, where you can just barely see the guy drifting in and out. You can be walking in and no one can see you, then there's a patch where they can see you.

Brother Dickey was sitting right close to the drive; one of the few drives that runs through the graveyard. He was sitting on a grave meditating, with his legs crossed and arms folded across his chest. He was wearing one of his gray karate outfits and had a gray band tied around his head that hung down around his shoulders. With his long, straight, dark hair and black Fu Manchu mustache; that would have been enough to scare anybody.

Well, this black man, an older gentleman with a thin build, was walking down the road. He was headed for the river, carrying a fishing pole over his shoulder and a can of worms in the other hand. He sees Dickey sitting on the grave with the fog around him looking like Fu Manchu. At the same time he sees Dickey — Dickey feels something and slowly turns his head to see the man.

Open the toilet, my man is gone. Fishing pole in one direction and can of worms in the other. Feets don't fail me now! Like Bullet Bob Hayes running the 100-yard dash, my man was outta there.

Like I said, I love this story. When Dickey told me what happened, I could see the whole thing. I'm sure he thought Dickey was coming up out of that grave, and I think that would have shaken my shit too. Especially if I was tripping! Get back!

The White Elephant
My First Road Trip

THE BAND'S SECOND ROAD trip was to New York City, the Big Apple. I had done a lot of things, but not this. This is my first, so I'm hyped. I drove the white elephant, an old Dodge van that was ready for the grave. We were north of Atlanta on Interstate 85 when Twiggs said, "Follow the signs to Greenville, South Carolina." And that's what I was doing, except I was so hyped that I read the Gainesville, Georgia cut off as Greenville. I saw the "G" and never looked any further. Now don't ask me how, but I can do that. So here we go headed for Gainesville.

I had only gone about five miles or so when Twiggs woke up and asked where we were. He must have sensed I messed up, but I just said, "We're headed for Greenville."

As soon as I said that, we saw a sign saying Gainesville.

Twiggs says, "Goddamn Red Dog. Turn on the light."

"Turn on the light," is a line that Twiggs and I had a lot of fun with for years. It was the way he said it, and we had many a laugh over it. It's one of those personal things. Like I had a word for him that surfaced about five or six years later. He used to love the ladies and would buy them things. One kind of took to him so I teased him by calling him MAMAMAMAMAAAAllet. I would holler it all over the stage, and sometimes over the mic during a roadie sound check.

Well, I "turned on the light," and Twiggs figured out what to do. So we were on our way for a while until the White Elephant blew up in Greenville, where we had to hang until we could rent a van. We were there all day then finally left for New York City sometime after dark.

Payne and Mike were in the truck, which was an old 12-foot Avis Rent-A-Truck that we got for $200, and another $300 to rebuild the engine. That truck ran forever making two trips to California and back, plus up and down the East Coast. The rest of us were packed in the Rent-A-Van. One person drove, one rode shotgun, and the rest to the rear.

We also had the guitars and suitcases with us. We slept on a mattress with our feet next to the heads of the person on each side. Now, if you were in the truck you had a little more room, but we had more dope in the van. So, now we're moving. We're high and we're happy. We're laughing with guitars playing and singing until the wee hours of the morning.

We got to NYC and no sooner got the rooms when Twiggs got into an argument with the front desk. We were thrown out not five minutes after we got there. So Beelzebub's shadow is with us from the start; not many gigs and things were starting to happen. No money; my disability check helped, but with stuff like this happening, all you could do was put your head down and stumble through it; starving and running stud service across the country.

Daytona Beach Interlude

THIS ONE TIME GREGG, Kim and I were in Daytona partying up. We used to go down to Daytona Beach a lot. Momma Allman lived there and we could stay at her house, just like we used to do when Berry's parents lived in Sarasota. It didn't make any difference which house we were at, there would be bodies all over the place. And I don't know how the parents put up with it, but they did with open arms.

Pam Roberts, the daughter of the great race car driver Fireball Roberts, was a good friend of Gregg's. She had a boyfriend, but her and Gregg sometimes did a thing on the side. So this one night, me, Gregg, Kim, Pam, her boyfriend and about three other people were sitting in the living room of a friend of Pam's. We were smoking and waiting for more dope when all of a sudden this guy comes running from the hallway. He stood in the living room and pointed a gun right at me. He yells, "Don't nobody move. Police." He was a plainclothes policeman. He was shaking, which made me think his gun was going to go off any minute, but I remained calm. Then he tells us he has a warrant for Pam's boyfriend, and more plainclothes policemen come in and take him away.

Now the only way the police could get in the house was through the bathroom window, and hell, I don't know how he got his fat ass through that little window.

Save the Bass

About the same time as Woodstock we were playing at Ungano's down in the Village. I think we played there a couple of nights, and what a dump. I'm sorry, but this place sucked. It had a lot of blacklights, and that strobe light. Try fixing something with the strobe light going. Hell, you can't keep up with your hand. Everything is done by feel. Like playing, just close your eyes and do it. And that's what Berry should have done; closed his eyes and played, because he walked right off the front of the stage.

You see Berry would walk around while he played. He moved all around the stage so he could hear what it sounded like all over. Now Brother Berry knew what it sounded like laying on his back about five feet below everybody else.

Save the bass. Above all else save the bass. That's the real roadie creed: Protect the instruments at all cost. Well, it's a good thing the Oak was a little messed up because it made him relax. He bounced and he didn't hurt himself, then got back up on stage like nothing ever happened, and we rocked on.

You know I'm amazed we did all this stuff and more. Plus it's all true. Now why did they use Meatloaf to play a roadie when they should have used me?

Pull Us Up Kim

"Pull us up Kim. Pull us up." That's what I was saying to Kim as he pulled Gregg and me up with this big crane. But let me back up a few hours.

It's about two in the morning and Kim, Gregg and myself were down in the Village boogying up. We are good and messed up. I mean we are rocking. For a group of guys with no money, we sure stayed messed up. People used to come up and give us stuff all the time.

We were broke, not a dime, and messed up on some side street. There was this mattress up against a building, so we sat down on the sidewalk and used the filthy mattress as a back and headrest. We didn't have any smokes and dying for a ready roll, so Kim reaches over and says, "Fuck it," as he picks up a cigarette butt from the sidewalk, and fires her up. Well, you know it's the blind leading the blind when me and my brothers drink wine. Now that's a line from a Paul Butterfield song I heard; except he said when me and my baby drink wine, so this was the blind leading the blind when brothers were drinking wine.

Well, Gregg and me did the same thing. While we are having a short smoke, we decide to whip out the johnsons and take a whiz and try to see who could reach the street, which we all did. Upon relieving ourselves we pulled our nasty asses up, grabbed another butt off the street, and moved on.

Now it's about four in the morning and we were close to the Holiday Inn around ninth and 51st streets. We were walking and just taking it easy. Nobody was around and the place was dead. We were going in for the night. You know the rooster crows at the early morning light, but some of us are calling it a night; that's a line from one of my songs.

Anyway, low and behold Payne sees this crane, a big crane sitting where a building used to be, so the three of us go over and Slim, that's Kim, jumps up, hotwires the crane, and lowers the hook on the end of the cable. When it gets to where we can reach it, both Gregg and me grabbed the hook, a big ass hook. Kim starts to pull us up, and Gregg drops off about six or seven feet up. But I hang on, and up I go, as Payne takes me out over the road and back, then back down as I'm hollering, "Yeah, ride em doggie! Ride em!" What a rush! Even if I was high. Just another day on the road, so we moved on to the hotel.

Target Practice

WE SEEMED TO DRAW the law like shit draws flies, but we were having fun. It wasn't too long after this when we were leaving Washington, D.C., from a gig the night before, and we got pulled over. We were about 30 miles down the road when the police pulled us and made us follow them back to the hotel.

Duane was into throwing knives for awhile, but he didn't have anything to throw at, so he used the headboard in the room as a target. And that headboard looked like shit; holes all in the thing, so we had to pay and they let us go. What can I say? The law was there again.

Happy Birthday Twiggs

IT WAS TWIGGS'S BIRTHDAY in 1969 when he told the band and crew to be at the playground of Alexander Ford Elementary School on the corner of Ridge Avenue and Drury Drive. He told us to be there at four in the afternoon, and we got there a little early, so we hung out at Twiggs's apartment, which was on the corner of Dreury across from the basketball courts.

At 4:00 p.m. exactly we were standing on the playground like he said, and there was a plane in the sky with Twiggs jumping out. He had a flare strapped to his lower right leg so we can see him free falling, sky diving, and it sure looked neat. Now that's one thing I couldn't do. I've done a lot of things, but that's one I don't think I want to do.

Anyway, Twiggs lands safely and we are all glad. We told him how neat it looked, which made him feel good, because he had an ego like the rest of us. We all like to do the best we can so we can let our ego out, and Twiggs was riding high. He should have been too, it was his birthday and it was something, one of those little things to bring this family together. We sure were happy then. Ten Rogues struttin' our stuff.

Kind Hearted Woman

MAMA LOUISE HUDSON. NOW what I can I say about this beautiful woman, the mother of the Allman Brothers Band. Of course we all had our real mothers, who were just great. I mean they are our moms, the main ladies in each of our lives. You know, the ones who are always there when you need them. However, this tail is about a lady that took the Allman Brothers under her wing and treated us like we were her sons. She was just as nice as she could be.

I think Phil Walden took Duane to the H & H Restaurant for lunch one day, then Duane took us all back in to eat sometime later. We didn't have much money so we would go every now and then, and we always went around the first of the month when my disability check came. For $1.25, you got a big leg and thigh of chicken fried up crispy, two vegetables, either collards, corn, rice, mashed potatoes and gravy, or butter beans, and a big jar of sweetened ice tea, or a big jar of the best lemonade in the world. Think about that, all for a $1.25.

When my disability check came I would give it to Twiggs and he would divide it up with the band; that's $92 divided by ten people. then if we got a gig, or somehow got our hands on a little money, Twiggs would pay me back. Then he would take it back again, like a revolving door trip, so I never did get paid back. There was no way you could get paid back. That money helped keep the band together.

Duane told me once that Dickey wasn't happy because we had very little money, and he was tired of being broke. Duane said my disability, and the check for $80 that Twiggs got from Phil every two weeks, which he also gave to the band, was helping keep us together. He said, "I just want to thank you, you're an Allman Brother." Now, the reason I mention this is because there's really no way to pay back Mama Louise for what she did, and I'll tell you why.

What little money we did have went to feed the babies; Vaylor, Brittany, and the wives, so we didn't go to the H&H for a while. We had moved into other apartments, but money was still at a low, so we ate beans twice a day. Then one day we all went down to the H & H, and Mama Louise said, "Where you been?"

I told her, "We don't have money."

Now by this time she has taken a liking to me, and of course the band, but she loves her Red Dog, so she says, "Don't you ever stay away from here because you ain't got no money."

Then she asked Duane if he wanted some butter, and Duane said, "Butter will put fat around your heart."

Mama Louise immediately fired back from behind the counter, "Red Dog, honey, don't you eat no butter," and we all laughed really hard.

After that she fed us for a year — for free. She fed the entire band, the wives, kids, and even some friends now and then. She even did the same thing for a few other bands. Sometimes I ate there three times a day. So how the hell could you ever pay her back? There's no way. If she wants to bring a hundred people to a gig, open the door. She is truly the mother of the Allman Brothers Band.

She would even get on you just like your mother. One time I went in to the H & H all messed up. I mean all you had to do was look at me and you could see I was rocking. Well Mama Hill, who was Mama Louise's partner in the H & H Restaurant, that's Hudson & Hill, is one of the sweetest ladies God ever put on this earth. When I went in she looked at me and just smiled, then Mama Louise fed me. When I finished eating she leaned over, hugged me and said in my ear, "Don't you ever come in that front door in this condition again. You come to the back." And she was right, I should have never gone in there like that, and that's what I did from then on. If I was buzzin,' I'd go to the back door, sit on the steps, and someone would bring me a plate of food and a big tea. I never even ordered. She just brought me what she thought I should eat. I love you, Mama Louise.

Christmas in New York

A COUPLE OF DAYS before Christmas of 1969 we were snowed in on the outskirts of Chicago. It was nighttime and the motel was, well, let's just say cheap. There was a big field behind it and somehow we all ended up in the field naked, running and diving in the snow with snowflakes falling on us. You know we were drunk, we were out of dope so we drank alcohol to act like dopes. At least dope mellows you out somewhat, where alcohol just makes you a dumbass all of the time.

The next morning we got out of there and headed for New York City to play the Fillmore East for the first time. We were in the white Ford van, basically an engine with wheels and tin around it. We had to put a piece of cardboard in front of the radiator when it was cold, and it was colder than a bitch now. There was snow on the ground from Chicago to New York, and all the cardboard did was generate enough heat on the driver's right foot, while the rest of you felt like ice. We had two people in the truck, and eight in the van laid up asshole to belly button, head to toe. So believe it when I say this was a rough trip, but we made it.

When we got to New York it was Christmas Eve, so we all cleaned up to have our first Christmas dinner together: The Preacher, the Deacon, and eight disciples. The meal with wine cost about $250 or more, and it took every dime we had. Twiggs even had to tell the waiter we didn't have enough money to give him a tip, but he said he would come back tomorrow and take care of him. Well, the waiter wasn't happy. He had just done a hell of a job. I mean to wait on this herd. Good luck! Twiggs did go back to the restaurant the next day however, and it blew the guy away. He just knew he would never see us again. Wrong, he didn't know Twiggs. If Twiggs took the time to say something, he did what he said.

Bill Graham had booked us for the gig without listening to the record. He had us on a bill with Blood, Sweat and Tears, and Dreams, which was a group formed in 1969 that included my good friend and great drummer Billy Cobham. The audience was mostly older people, and I saw quite a few gray heads, but I tell you what, they were moving when we played. We got encores and standing ovations all three nights.

Bill knew he had put us with the wrong band. That was the first time he ever booked a band without listening to their music, and he said he would never do it again. However, on this gig it didn't make any difference. The band was hot and he fell in love with us. The whole stage crew, and everybody associated with the Fillmore did. We eventually played the Fillmore about thirteen times or so, and became Bill's favorite band. He was also our favorite promoter, and his shows were the best. He laid out a spread like nobody.

The Fillmore was the place to play. There's nothing like it, even today. The crew was the best I have ever seen, and I've seen a lot. They had everything together and expected you to have your stuff together, which we did. Twiggs blew them away. He called the lights and was on top of it. He had their mouths open.

Bill was also known to correct mistakes, and he had us right back in February to play with the Grateful Dead for two nights. That was our kind of crowd, and our kind of people to play with. I believe the band Love, which was another damn good band, also played, but the main thing Bill did was bring together the best band from the West and the best band from the East.

What music was played between those walls. On the last show the Dead and Brothers would join at the end, and that was unreal. I was tripping on good liquid acid and hitting the laughing gas. Some friends of the Dead had a tank of it back stage in one of the dressing rooms which were really small. Just to describe it for a second, since it was the Fillmore; there were about two rooms to a floor from the second floor up. A spiral staircase that you went up, and there weren't any at stage level.

Some of the old ladies who were there got pissed at me because they saw this girl Suzie give me head up against the wall backstage, but what was I supposed to say? No? The trouble is they forget how they get your ass to begin with, and believe me they weren't acting like Lady Jane. There ain't a musician's wife, a ball player's wife, a doctor's or lawyer's wife that didn't give up something first, and give up something good. They have to lay the trap. If they didn't, they were playing a game like; I don't want to be like those other girls, I want you to respect me. Great, this sounds good, but it's the trap, because as soon as you marry them — bang — they're out giving it to whoever wants it. Then they say; I was drunk and it just happened. Well the rose doesn't get dew on it without some kind of thought pattern.

I took Suzie back to the hotel and did more Red Dog things. Then I was asleep when I woke up being bounced up and down on the bed. Hell, it was Mike with Suzie. We were about four to a room, so either you had to watch or take part, and Mike chose to take part, being that he didn't have any and he's a brother. I did a thing with Suzie for a year or so. When we were in New York we used to walk down the street with one arm around each other, and our hand in each other's back pockets playing with the other's ass.

Drawing at the Chelsea

I KNOW SOMEBODY OUT there remembers the Crawdaddy Newspaper, that's what I call it anyway, a newspaper like Rolling Stone, with rock news and a little more.

Well right after the first album came out, we were staying at the Chelsea Hotel, and we were able to get three or four rooms now, but that was at the Chelsea. There was Duane, Berry, Butch, Mike Callahan, Kim Payne, and me, and everybody else was just coming and going. Hell, I guess we were all coming and going out of that room, which was Duane and Berry's.

This reporter from Crawdaddy was there and had a photographer with him. He was interviewing Duane, and everyone was quick drawing with Twiggs's Colt .44 cap and ball pistol, which was the real thing. Twiggs's hand made this beautiful cowboy belt and holster, so everyone would put it on and quick draw. I remember helping Twiggs make the holster. We stayed up a few night working, and me helping. You know, "Hold this Augie," as I say laughing about it now. He would make a mistake, then start all over. One time he was almost finished and made a mistake. Then he pissed, bitched and moaned, and took it apart and started all over again. It had to be perfect for him, and if you knew Twiggs you know what I'm saying, he was a perfectionist.

Anyway, everyone would put on the gun and holster and see who could draw the fastest. That was Duane, Dickey, and Butch. I think Dickey had the edge, but I'm not sure because all three were really fast.

This reporter from Crawdaddy was sitting on the bed with Duane, leaning back against the headboard as I was jumping around, up and down, on the bed and off the bed, just being Red Dog. Now, while I was doing this I was quick drawing. I would jump up on the bed next to Duane, turn around, and draw Twiggs's Colt — bang, bang — and I had on this black cowboy hat of Twiggs's, which was the same one he's wearing in the picture on the back of Fillmore East album.

I'm proud to say that picture was my idea. When we got the proofs back Twiggs was staying in Buffalo, so I told Duane it would be neat if we could put a picture of Twiggs on the back cover; up above the road crew so it would look like a picture hanging on your wall, like in your living room. I loved Twiggs and I said, "Just because he is away, he is still a brother, and it would make him feel better."

Duane said, "Augie, that's a good idea," but I never heard another word about it. Then the album came out and there was Brother Twiggs.

I was also wearing Brother Mike's poncho, which looked like the one Clint Eastwood wore in the movies like Fistful of Dollars. You see with my hair to my shoulders and my beard, I looked like this tough cowboy. I didn't know until Duane told me later, but the reporter asked Duane, "Who the hell is that?"

Now you have to know that Duane said he was going to make me a legend. If I was out on stage fixing something and the song ended he would always announce me as Legendary Red Dog.

Then Brother Duane turned and looked the reporter straight in the eye and said, "You don't know who that is?"

The reporter said, "No."

With a smile Duane replied, "That's the Legendary Red Dog." With this, the Crawdaddy dude goes to writing and motions to the photographer to start taking pictures.

The next time we went to New York City and stayed at the Chelsea, Berry called me on the phone and told me to come over to his and Duane's room. When I got there they showed me the issue of Crawdaddy with pictures of the band. Well I'm looking through it and each picture of a band member is about four inches by four inches. Then there's a picture that takes up half the page, which looks to me like Twiggs, until I read the caption underneath and it says, "The Legendary Red Dog of the Allman Brothers Band."

I said, "What?" I didn't know how to act. I just looked at Duane and Berry and said, "I love you guys."

Talking about Crawdaddy, I think it was them who got a hold of the pictures from the first album. The one shot in the creek on Otis Reddings's place in the country, outside of Macon. The one that shows everyone in the band naked and sitting except for Butch who is standing. Of course, in those days we liked to go naked, we would shed clothes like a bad habit, but the reason Butch is standing is because he cut his knee while we were making my armband. You know the old hippie arm bands we all wore? We had this leather kit when we lived at 309 College Street; that's where ten of us lived in a one-room apartment, in a building that should fall down. Butch was cutting this hole in my armband when the blade slipped and went right across his leg, right above his knee. Deep. So now you know the big secret, he couldn't get his knee in the creek. And remember that first orgy? Well, this picture was during the day, and the orgy was the same night.

Anyway, Bill Graham got a copy of the picture from Crawdaddy that shows the band standing up naked in the creek. He blew it up to a little larger than life-size, and hung it on the wall right across from the concession counter at the Fillmore East. Well, hell. Now everyone in the world knows what our johnsons look like, so maybe that's why we got so much rose.

This is also when I met Carol Green. She worked the concession counter, and gave me a night I never forgot. I don't know where she is, but I'll say I love you Carol. I hope your journey through the darkness of time is rewarding.

Tail at the Chelsea
Song For the Ladies

WE WERE STAYING AT the Chelsea Hotel in the Big Apple, and had Sister Jane and a lady friend of hers in the room. I was getting a little lip while everyone was watching, but I wasn't responding, so Sister Jane told her friend, "Get out of the way, this is mine, you don't know what you're doing." She said, "Watch I'll show you how to get things moving," and that's exactly what she did.

As soon as Elmoe got to pointing she stopped and looked at her friend and said, "I told you this was mine," then she went right back to taking care of business.

A little later I was using a long neck wine bottle on Jane's friend, and got my face real close to her so I could get a good look at the action when her rose opened up. It was a gusher all over my face. I never had that happen, and it was great. Stud service one way or another. They didn't call us freaks for nothing.

That reminds me of when we met Sweet Connie Climax. Her mom had taken her to Memphis to get her away from a band that was coming to Little Rock. They checked into the same hotel as us and Sweet Connie found the Coyote right off the bat, so away they went. A little while later he called and said she was too much for one man, so we all filed in. Now some people might say they didn't play, but I saw the book she kept, and it had everybody's name from our band listed, plus everyone she had been with that was in a band. If you did a good job she put a star next to your name, and I had two stars beside mine. I just talked to the man sailing the boat, and that's why I had two stars.

Sweet Connie was, and she still is a hell of a nice person. She just likes to make love and so do I. What can I say? She gave us the services we desired, and that's how we met the Lady of Rock and Roll. Love ya' Connie.

Most bands today, and that's the musicians and all the road people, look at the ladies of the highway; the groupies, like they are pieces of shit. They badmouth them and call them names like bimbo. Shit man, if you aren't getting laid you aren't a happy camper. It helps keep your shit together. When you're happy you work better, so why the hell do you want to badmouth the ladies that give you the rose on the highway?

So here's a song for the ladies of the road:

Good Time Lady

Good time lady
Sweet, sweet lady
I need your love oh so bad
It gives me the strength
To go down the road and sing this song

Good time lady
Sweet, sweet lady
I need your love oh so bad
I hear you cry
Walk on in
The good times are here again

Good time lady
Sweet sweet lady
I need your love, oh so bad
Hello, goodbye
Yes it's me I'm up and gone again
I'll be coming your way
I don't know when

Good time lady
Sweet, sweet lady
Please cry out
Walk on in
Sweet, sweet lady

Have you ever noticed how if one person is real happy, and bounces around kidding with everyone, that someone wants to bust their bubble by saying something that will embarrass you or put you down? These assholes are so jealous, they can't handle you getting the attention when they aren't. They need to loosen up and have more fun. You don't have to do drugs or alcohol, but you sure as hell can get some rose, laugh, joke, and tell bullshit stories like these. Most bands today seem to secure themselves away from the rose. These road people of today have an excuse; why for this or that, but that's like assholes, everybody's got one.

I used to go in the audience and give out back stage passes to the ladies. Now there's a trick to this, you have to pick all kinds; tall, short, fat, and skinny. That gives you a variety to choose from. If the gig was sold out, I would go to the back door and let however many people that were there in for free. I would do this right after the show started. I was just having fun and taking care of the mushroom people — for they are taking care of us, thank goodness.

Rockin' the House

AT THE TIME OF this next tail, we had three apartments; one on Bond Street where Duane and Donna lived, and two on Orange Street in the yellow house, a big house that had been turned into apartments.

Berry lived upstairs in the yellow house with Big Linda and their daughter, Brittany, who is my godchild. Butch and Momma Trucks lived downstairs, and we all crashed at one of the three apartments. Whichever one you were at when you fell out is where you slept.

One day Duane and Donna left Macon to go to Florida on a weekend trip. That left the apartment on Bond Street to Gregg, Kim, Dickey and me. The first night Duane and Donna were gone, the four of us went out and copped some Duji. That shit was bad too. I mean ferocious. We were back at the apartment when Kim fired up then passed out. We thought he was just laying back, but then Dickey got off and the same thing happened to him, then Gregg got me off because I wouldn't put the needle in my arm. Then he got off and passed out too, but for some reason, I didn't go out right away. I was so friggin' high but I knew something was wrong. We were lying all over the kitchen floor and I had Gregg's head in my lap, slapping him on the face saying, "Wake up, Bro. Wake up," but I couldn't hit very hard. I was doing good just to pick my arm up. The next thing I knew I woke up on the couch, but whenever I moved my head I threw up, so I just laid there real still.

Poochie and Chank had come by to see us, or they may have heard we copped and wanted to come by for a taste. The door was open when they got there so they came on in. It's a good thing they did too, like I said we were all out cold, lying all over the kitchen floor. Poochie and Chank shot us up with saltwater by skin-popping, that's just a regular shot in the shoulder. Kim Dickey and me came out of it right away, but Gregg wouldn't respond, so they did it again, but still no response. Then Poochie mainlined Gregg with the saltwater, and he came around. Now we are all awake, or maybe I should say alive, but not awake. We kept nodding out and coming back, then nodding out again, and well, you know, that's why we did the stuff in the first place. The next day, for several days later, and maybe even weeks later you could feel death creeping around you. The apartment always seemed to be dark after that. Even with the sunlight coming in.

We made sure we crashed somewhere else when Duane and Donna got back on Sunday night. Then about four days later we went to Tampa to play at the University of South Florida. That was back when they held concerts in the old gym. Gregg had a nice abscess on his left arm where one of the saltwater shots had been administered, so Kim and me took him to the university hospital where they took care of him, but they also called the police. So when the police got there they talked to us, and I think they knew what was up, but couldn't prove anything. We weren't holding.

At the gig I made up ten one-gallon jugs of Gatorade. I put liquid acid in each one, and a strip of duck tape on each of the bottles. I wrote on the tape, "Take two swallows and pass it on." I had ten gallons of Electric Gatorade and dosed the whole place including the band, my sister Terry Lee for her first trip, and my cousin Debbie. Once again we rocked the house, electric style, but no matter what condition you were in, the gig came first — always first — the name of the game was the gig, and one can never forget his responsibilities.

The Love Children

The Fargle girls of Gainesville, Florida; I'll say right now these are four of the sweetest ladies around. They were bad! Until this day they are my friends. I love and respect them very much, and I'll cherish them in my heart forever. We sure as hell had some great times together. One of them was a friend of Duane and Gregg, and that's how we all met. If we were on our way to Miami with a couple days to hang, we could go to their apartment in Gainesville and lay up. It might be all of us, or maybe just one or two of us; either way they would always open up their apartment to us.

One time when Duane and I went down from Macon, Alan Walden gave us $100 to buy him some hash . No, don't give two hippies $100 to buy dope, because when we got there that was the first thing we did. We already bought wine on the way into town, but for the dope we had to settle for an ounce of Kief, which was the same type of high you get from hash and pot. We bought Allen an ounce, and I think we paid $40, then spent the other $60 on food to put in the apartment. That way we had enough for six people for three days.

We were drinking wine, smoking pot, and decided to try this Kief to make sure it was good. Well, that was the end of that. One hit led to another and three days later we headed back home to Macon with no money and no Kief. Allen wasn't a happy camper either. He tried to be cool, but we knew he was pissed.

One of the times all ten of us were there we were tripping and just hanging out. We were sitting around talking when I think it was Kim who decided he was going to take a bath. Well that's when things got good, real good. Kim was taking a bath in one of those old style tubs that sits on four legs when one of the Fargle girls went in to wash his back. Then all of a sudden there were two in the tub, then three in the tub, four in the tub, and the next thing you know we're all over the apartment. On the table, on the porch, in the beds, that was one hell of a night. All for one and one for all. The brotherhood strikes again, and the love children were on the move.

One day Payne, Callahan and me were in the equipment truck coming back from Miami headed for Macon. This is one of the times we were enjoying the fruits of our labor. We had these two lovely ladies with us, you know, Florida girls with nice tans and young bodies that talk to you. What can I say? I was talkin' my ass off.

As a matter of fact we, all five of us, were naked in the cab of the truck. Now picture this, five people in a cab was tight. It was a close fit for three people, and it was tight. So while Payne was driving we had to make things a little more comfortable. Callahan and me started lovin' the ladies, and I was in the middle with one sitting on Elmoe. Now I'm going to tell you why men name their buddy; they don't want no stranger leading them around. I just picked Elmoe, hard and dumb, but he points real well. Anyway, my man Callahan was doing the same thing with the other lady, and I was using the gear shift knob as a little stimulation on the other when we came to the last tollbooth on the Florida Turnpike. Payne pulled up to the booth and gave the guy money, the attendant gave Payne the change and the receipt, so Payne drives off. The whole time the guy never moved his head, he didn't even blink, not a word. But, his mouth opened wide to match the size of his eyes — he takes money and gives money. We just sat there as cool as ever looking right at him and kept right on. We thought for awhile he might turn us in, but we never got pulled or anything. You know, five hippies doing it in a truck, hell with it. We worked hard — we played hard, and I'll bet the guy has told this story even more than I have.

Roadies have to get a little rose where they can because you work your ass off. It's usually three or four in the morning when you have to head for the next gig, so that makes a quickie at the gig nice. You work better, and you're in a better mood. You know, you are up in more ways than one, I say laughing. Hard work, great music, and a little rose, what more can you ask for? That spells fun. Enjoying the fruits of our labor.

The People's Roadie

DURING SHOWS, I USED to like to let people get places on stage where they could see. I can just about run a stage in my sleep, and that's why I'm the number one roadie in the world. I know how to run a stage. One of the things Twiggs taught me was to think ahead. Like if you move a piece here, then six moves later will you have to move it again. That's the way he said it, "Think six moves ahead."

The trick is to be able to do everything while the band is playing, and with lots and lots of people on stage. Sometimes wall-to-wall people like the time in Chapel Hill, North Carolina. We were playing in a field by the side of the football field where they had a portable stage just big enough for us to fit on. The football field had a track around it with stands on the side, so to get in we had to drive the truck on the track, then turn through this gate, which was a tight fit. Tuffy gassed the truck slowly through the gate with just a few inches on each side.

We did the gig, and everyone was just raging on liquid acid. I know because I dosed the entire band. People were wall-to-wall, and standing right up against the amp line. Hell, they couldn't see a thing. The speaker cabinets were right in front of their faces. In those days, Butch and Jaimoe looked like two Cobras playing together and off of each other when they played the drums. They would be set up in front of the amp line, and had wall-to-wall, six to seven-foot high speaker cabinets behind them.

There were only a few places you could see through. Most people on stage couldn't see at all, but they could hear and feel the vibration of the stage. Well, somebody kicked out a speaker cord and I had to side step my way, squeezed against the backs of the cabinets, and face to face with the people to get to the trouble spot. When I got there with my legs kind of turned sideways, and from the waist up facing the people, while doing a squat with my back straight, I couldn't t see. I'd have to reach down and find the speaker cord and plug it back in. Then get up and say thank you for the few inches they gave, side step out of there, and go back to boogying. Like I said, try to do this and a lot of other shit while tripping.

We have played too long at the gig, but that was okay, we just had to shit and get. Everybody else flew but Tuffy and me. I was driving the Easy Ryder, and Tuffy was riding shotgun. It sounded like a tank because it didn't have a muffler, but I put the pedal to the metal and leapt out of there. Tuffy was about to lose it. The gate was right there and I drove through like lightning, never touching a thing. I just looked over and told Tuffy, "That's how you drive motherfucker," as I say laughing about it now, and we headed for the Big Apple late Saturday or early Sunday morning — whatever you want to call it. We had two more gigs to get two, one at 138th Street and Amsterdam at one in the afternoon, and one at Hofstra University in Hempstead, New York at eight o'clock the same night.

On the way up Interstate 95 between Richmond, Virginia and Washington, D.C., the alternator arm broke right in half. Now we didn't realize this was the problem. We were still tripping, but it looked like it was getting foggy outside, so I said, "Where the hell is this fog coming from?" It was getting thicker and thicker and we could hardly see each other. Then I realized it wasn't fog at all, it was smoke, so I said, "Shit Bro, we're on fire. That's not fog, that's smoke."

Tuffy started to pull over, and I said, "What are you doing?"

He said, " I'm pulling over," and I said, "No, we have to keep going. We can't leave the truck on the road with the gear in it." That's a real roadie's number one rule: Gear first above life.

I saw some lights in the distance, and said, "Head for those lights."

Then out of nowhere, just like it came out of the dark, an exit pops up. We almost missed our chance, but we made it off of the interstate.

I said, "Head for that gas station," the only thing that was open. We had to get the truck there no matter what. Stay with the ship — she is still running.

Now you're not going to believe this. That gas station was the only place open for ten miles either way, and the only person working was a six-foot tall white woman; a country lady that knows her shit. Well, Tuffy and her found what the problem was and rigged the arm so we could continue on. Then they disappeared around the corner. They slipped and slid for a while, and we were back on the road. See how we had a knack for finding a little? Even out in the middle of nowhere.

We finally met up with the band in New Jersey, but we were late, and everybody was getting worried we might have had a wreck. We made it with time to tell the story and leave for the first gig, but no time for sleep — take another hit of acid. We pulled the gigs off great. We were a little late for the Hofstra gig, but that was because we didn't get to play the first gig until about 4 or 5 p.m.

First Run of the Winny

WE HAD JUST GOT the Winnebago and I was officially hired to be the driver. I was actually hired while we were in the process of buying the Winnebago. We were at the Georgian Terrace Hotel in Atlanta, when Duane sent word for me to come to the dressing room, which was just a regular hotel room. I had just dropped Berry's bass on the street and thought for sure I was in trouble. But to my surprise, in front of everyone else he said, "You are officially hired to be the driver of the Winnebago," which lit me up like a Christmas tree. I forgot all about dropping Berry's bass until he went to play it and it was out of tune. Then I told him what happened, and thank God, nothing was wrong except for it being out of tune.

The first gig after we got the Winny was in Philly at the Electric Factory. We were at the gig, parked across the street, and it was colder than hell and snowing, when just before the show the toilet backs up. It needed to be emptied, so we had positioned the Winny by a street drain.

I went out to empty the shit tank, and kiss my ass the friggin' dump line is frozen, so I got a fork off the Winny and went to chopping. I chopped and chopped about a foot up the tube to where it took a 90 degree turn to the left. I chopped through the turn and then it happened. Just as I made a small hole, the whole thing broke loose. It went down my arm, hit my armpit, and went down my side. Here it is colder than hell, and I've got shit and piss all over me, so I run on into the camper. She was full of people, but I didn't have any trouble getting by. They all moved right out of the way like the parting of the Red Sea. You could smell me coming. Then I cleaned up, we did the gig, got high, got a little rose, and headed for San Francisco to play a gig at the Fillmore West.

It was daylight, still snowing and cold, but we were moving along and making pretty good time. Sometime before noon, Butch started cooking a pancake breakfast, and they sure as hell were good. I'll tell you, one thing Trucksey can do is burn. I mean the man can cook. The pancakes were light and fluffy, and it was the first meal prepared in the Winny. This was great. Hip at that time. We were all together, headed for the gig and eating at the same time. The smell of food in the Winny and the snow outside just seemed to make it all the better.

While we were eating Twiggs said, "We got two girl hitchhikers up here."

So we all said in loud voices, "Pick 'em up. Pick 'em up."

Now never let it be said that we passed up a little on the road, so that's exactly what brother Twiggs did. He picked them up. Well guess who it was? It was Sister Jane and her lady friend who we originally met in New York about a month before. We had just seen them last night at our gig in Philly, and they were hitchhiking in the snow to California to see us at the Fillmore.

Now we have it like we wanted. We're in a 27-foot camper with food, get high, beer, a couple ladies to keep us company, and we're going to the gig. All for one and one for all.

After traveling for a while we got around Cincinnati and the wipers stopped working. Twiggs was driving, so he stopped to fix them. He worked on them for about two or three hours and Twiggs being Twiggs did not want to give up. He was a perfectionist. Do I need to say more? If he said "We are leaving at eight o'clock," that's what he meant, not 8:01. But now he's very pissed, he can't fix the wipers, and won't leave until finally Duane tells him, "Let's go."

The next night I was tripping on acid somewhere around 2 a.m. when Twiggs is riding beside me going over the electric system. He did this because I would fill the water tank of the Winny but the water wouldn't last long, and we would run out.

Twiggs had explained to me before how to fill the tank. First you hook up the water hose to Winny, then turn off the water pump, then open up the overflow valve which would relieve the pressure in the water tank so it could fill up.

If you didn't turn the pump off, the pressure stayed in the tank and the tank would not fill up. It acted like it was full, and water came out of the overflow line, but the pressure wouldn't let the tank fill. Now that's all the steps there were, then turn the water on.

Well this is exactly what I was doing, except I was forgetting to turn off the pump and the water would run out real quick. The toilet would start to stink and Twiggs would say, "Augie did you fill the tank?"

I'd say, "Yes."

The next time, the same thing, and he would say, "Did water come out the overflow line?"

I said, "Yes, water came out the overflow line."

Until about the fourth time he said, "Show me exactly what you are doing." So I showed him.

He shit, "No wonder there's no fuckin' water Augie. You got to turn off the pump," and he explained the whole routine over. Twiggs was like that.

Like I was saying this time Twiggs was going over the electric system starting at the battery. He would explain a little bit, then ask me some questions. If I missed one he would start all over again. So now I'm tripping, driving, and being quizzed on the electric system all at the same time, but after that night I knew the Winny from front to back.

You see I missed a lot of questions, and I have to be honest, I thought I knew something. You know how you are in your 20s? You think you got it, but you don't. I was just a happy-go-lucky kid having fun, and Twiggs actually took me under his wing and taught me a lot. One hell of a lot. He taught me how to work and have fun, and that the job always came first.

I sure miss him. I remember when we were coming home after the Buffalo deal. We were on the Baltimore Beltway, and I was driving with Duane sitting beside me when tears started to come down my cheeks just a little. Duane saw this and says, "What's wrong with you Augie?"

I said, "Ah man, we shouldn't have left Twiggs. We should have stayed and tried to get him out."

Duane said, "I thought you didn't like Twiggs."

I said, "Big Bro, I love him. I know we argue a lot, but that doesn't mean anything. Twiggs taught me too good. We argued because I thought my way was right, and Twiggs liked that. He said it showed I was thinking." Of course Twiggs would always win because he was always right, but Duane never said another word about it. He just reached over and patted me on the back a couple of times, then played some nice blues on his acoustic guitar.

That's one thing that made the trips nice. Someone would always ride shotgun and play. Everybody might be sleeping and I would be driving with Duane, Berry, or Dickey sitting beside me late at night playing. I could drive all night like that, and that's what I would do. Drive.

Well, after my electric lesson Twiggs went to bed and I was still tripping when we get to the top of the mountains coming into Albuquerque, New Mexico. Where we were you could look down and see the city, and all the different colored lights. You know how neon lights look? Well there were a lot of them, and this was one pretty sight, so I pulled the Winny over and woke everyone up, "Look at this, it's beautiful." And it was, if you were tripping.

But, I don't think everybody saw it like me, "Yes, Red Dog. That's pretty. Don't wake us up again," and they went back to sleep, as I proceeded to drive the Winny right down the mountain. What a difference a little tripping makes (laughing).

The next day Mike and Kim were in the truck and the rest of us in the Winny when we got separated. We got into Flagstaff and started to run low on gas so we had to make a decision. If we filled up now it should get us to San Francisco or close. We had just enough money to fill the tank, and enough money left over to buy a case of beer because we were out. Or, we could keep the money and not buy beer in case we needed to get more gas. Well, I'll tell you one must get his priorities together. That was no choice. We bought the case of beer.

At dark we pulled off and stopped along side the road about 50 miles on the other side of Flagstaff. Butch was fixing supper, and we weren't there five minutes it seemed when the door of the Winny flew open and in walked Payne and Callahan. They found us way out in the middle of nowhere. They must have smelled the beer because they were out too. They only had enough money in the truck fund to make it to San Francisco. The girls got out and headed for L.A. saying they would see us there. Now we're happy because we are all together again. No rose, and we are out of everything, but we got beer and were moving on.

We stopped at the Grand Canyon. What a neat place no matter how many times you see it. Twiggs took a bunch of pictures of everyone climbing around having fun. We used to do that, just stop and check things out, and it made trips more enjoyable.

We made it to San Francisco, but now we didn't have money for the toll to get across the bridge. All that great planning we did and now they have to throw a toll on us. What the hell to do? Get out and panhandle? Can you see Berry Oakley telling this girl who just stopped to pay her toll that he is the bass player with the Allman Brothers Band, and we are playing the Fillmore West? Yep, that's right.

"Why are you asking me for a handout?" and Berry goes into his act.

He could talk you out of your shirt if he wanted. Well, the girl felt sorry for him and paid the toll for us, so he invited her to the gig, but she never showed up that I know of.

That gig with Hot Tuna at the Fillmore was great. Jack Casady and Berry got together and did a lot of rapping about basses. When they started jamming in the dressing room, I got the same feeling watching them as I did seeing Duane and Clapton. It could bring tears to your eyes, and was very heavy. Two masters of their instruments. In fact just being at the Fillmore West was very intense for me, and this was icing on the cake.

Afterwards we partied up and headed for L.A. We parked the Winny at a house where two lady friends of Kim and Gregg lived. Some of us stayed in the house and the rest of us stayed in the Winny. Our good friend Larry "Rhino" Reinhardt from the Gray House in Jacksonville was now playing lead for Iron Butterfly. He also lived in L.A. at this time, so we hooked up with him. Rhino put us in touch with the right man to get what we needed head wise, and we spent three or four days in LA until we headed home to Macon.

The trip home was a lot different than the trip to California where there was a lot of smoke, acid, and booze going on. Coming home was nod time. It took three days and three nights of continuous driving because we had a big bag of pot, hash, three hundred reds, and are you ready for this? Sixteen pints of Robitussin AC cough syrup. So we drank some AC right off the bat to get ready for the long haul.

On long runs like this everybody would drive a little, but the main drivers were still me and Twiggs in the Winny, and Mike and Kim in the truck. Everyone took their spots for the trip, and Jaimoe took his position in the hallway. The hallway was about two feet wide, and he stood with his back against one wall and his head barely touching the other wall. Let's say there were brief moments when "Frown" wasn't standing right there in that spot, but my man had a great nod going. I wished I could have joined him, but I had to drive, so I'd be working on my nod while I drove. When I got relieved I could jump right into it. Which is exactly what I would do, and believe me there was a lot of nodding going down.

You see no matter if we were coming or going there was never a dull moment. After the end of the run the Winny was broke in Allman Brothers style.

This makes me think of going through the Smoky Mountains at daylight. We were coming out of Knoxville tripping, and I was driving the Winny while Kim Payne was driving the truck with Mike riding shotgun. How far out of Knoxville we were I don't know, but I do know the road was under construction. They had those little orange reflectors everywhere. I mean it was like being surrounded.

We were rolling along, fucking around with each other, and I got about as close as I could to the truck. I must have been about ten feet away from the back when Payne said to Mike, "Watch this."

You see the road did a real sharp curve to the left, and Payne didn't touch the brake at all, so there were no lights to let me know something was getting ready to happen. Like him making the sharp curve and me all of a sudden looking at piles of dirt. I turned the Winny real hard and somehow made the turn, but now everybody is on the floor. I just threw the band out of their beds and hollered back, "It's okay, it's okay. Go back to sleep."

Well I don't know how, but everyone did go back to sleep. Take another pill — no way, not us. A little while later I made Payne pull over and asked him, "What the hell are you doing? My heart is in my ass."

He was laughing so hard, and said, "I knew it would open you up, and I knew you could handle it."

I started laughing and said, "Man you should see what I did. Not one, but I threw the whole band on the floor, and they were all hollering at me." I told Payne and Mike, I knew we were history. We laughed some more and went on down the road.

Right after daylight, we are dead in the middle of the Smoky Mountains. Remember now, I was tripping and this looked freaky. It was the first time I ever saw the Smokies and I thought this is great. So once again I pulled the Winny over and yelled out, "Everybody up! Everybody up! You got to see this," and I got off the Winny.

Everyone followed me, but now they could throw me off the mountain for waking them up. They all got back in pissing and moaning, I got back behind the wheel, and started moving on down the road. All the while mumbling, "I don't know why you guys have to get pissed. It's smoke coming out of the mountains and it looks great. I like it."

Berry said, "Well, like it while you are driving. And don't stop." He headed to his bed laughing, so I keep driving through the Smokies and believe it, it was one beautiful sight. Tripping wasn't a bad way to see the Smokies.

Let me explain about tripping and driving. The first thing is, do not to take a four way, take one-fourth. This way you get off just enough and things don't move on you. Things just look more intense and you are in a state of awareness, if you know what I mean. Like you could see through the b.s., like tell when someone was lying, like the antenna stands high. That's what awareness was, and I always saved a part of the trip to be with the spirits.

Now don't get the wrong idea, one does not go to the cosmos when driving. One must maintain, keep cool, and trip on down the highway. I'm lucky I guess. When I was driving and tripping things were always straight, but stop and things could get to moving on you. Then I would say "I'm tripping and this is neat," and everything straightened right up.

Of course I've had some experience at this. I tripped for two weeks. I started day one with one drop of acid, two drops the next day, and so on. You would build up a resistance so you had to increase the drops, but this kept me in a state of awareness. It was beautiful and the world looked great to this flower child. I escaped all the b.s., the war, the government, and big business. I was just a flower child floating in the wind. Just floating in the wind.

Leaving Jaimoe

I THINK WE WERE on our way to a gig in upstate New York when we took a shortcut from the D.C. Beltway to get over to the Baltimore Beltway. There was a little restaurant on the side of the road, so we stopped to eat breakfast. Now, while we are eating Jaimoe was out talking to some split tail on the payphone by the side of the road and the Winny was right beside the payphone. Now you got to understand, Jaimoe is basically a quiet person. He could be in a room and you would not know he is there, he just blends in.

So, we all come out of the restaurant right past Jaimoe, get in the Winny, and Twiggs says, "Are we all here?"

Somebody said, "Yes," and away we went.

Then we're on the Baltimore Beltway about halfway around when Duane said, "Where is Jaimoe?" No, he actually said, "Where is Frown?"

Oh shit, kiss my ass, we've left Jaimoe right there on the phone. So back we go to get him, and there he is standing beside the payphone. This is not the first time we left the La Moe Jai.

One time we left him sitting in the closet with the door shut, he used to do that so he could enjoy his nod. We were in Frisco playing the Fillmore West, and we were staying out in Sausalito. Hell, we had gotten over the bridge before we realized we left him. That was the first time we left him and not to be the last. But this did freak us out. We couldn't believe we went off and left him. Even if he was sitting in the closet with the door shut, we should have checked. That was Brother Jaimoe, and we all felt a little protective towards him, especially the roadies.

I mean Jaimoe was the only black brother in the band. We saw no color, but we sure knew that other people outside of the family didn't look at it that way. We were always a little on guard for someone to mess with him, and we got messed with a lot because we were a band of gypsies. You know what 1969 and the early 70s were like. If you were smart you didn't go anywhere by yourself. But you see, we have each other. The Brotherhood. All for one, one for all.

My First Bike

I ALMOST BOUGHT THE farm one night after I got my first bike, a 350 Honda. Duane wouldn't let me get anything bigger. He said I had to learn to ride first, but he picked out a 350 Honda that was beefed up for hill climbing.

About a week after I got the bike, Duane and me were out riding around Macon looking for some shit. After we copped, we headed home. We were about three or four blocks from the big house when the traffic light turned red as Duane shot through. Thank goodness the first car going in the opposite direction came to a full stop at the light where Vineville Avenue is four lanes. This car is in the inside lane, and I followed Duane. The road was wet, and there were two cars in front of me, one in each lane, so I opened the throttle up and skeet right between them. Well, as I got right in front of them, I lost her. I was already holding on for dear life, but shit, ballsy me, I was going through or else. Well, it was the "or else" and she went down.

The bike ended up in the middle of the intersection and I ended up, get this, with my head right in line with the driver's side wheels and just under the car. That's the car that had already stopped for the light going in the opposite direction. My body was sticking out in the road. As soon as I realized I was alive I jumped up and grabbed the bike. I never took her out of gear, and pushed her right out of the road. I was pushing her down the sidewalk towards the big house, and I have to push my ass off. Have you ever pushed a motorcycle that is in gear without pulling the clutch handle in? Fuck me, I'm so hyped up I thought the bike was messed up. That that's why it was so hard to push. I'm freakin' — I almost got killed.

Well Duane got home and I wasn't behind him, so he just knew something was wrong. He wouldn't come back to see, so he sent Kim and Mike. They came up shitting in their pants asking, "What happened, what happened?" and I tell them.

They said, "Are you ok?"

I said I was fine.

Payne said, "You dumbass. No wonder it's hard to push. You've got to take the damn thing out of gear." So we all laughed, and when we got home I told Duane what happened. He started telling me I can't follow him like that. But I said, "Where you go I go."

The good spirit of the hound was definitely hanging around that night.

The Green Weenie

ABOUT 3 MONTHS LATER I bought a 650 Triumph Bonneville. I put a 750 Route kit, an E.T. ignition on her, and painted her green. Everyone said green was bad luck on a motorcycle, and that's the first thing I did. I called her the Green Weenie and she was fast. Four wires on the whole bike — light and fast — The Green Weenie.

Now we really started to ride. Ride fast and wild like a cowboy on a wild bronco. That was the only way I had to get around. So when I was home that's what I did, ride and get a little rose. Sometimes I did both at the same time. What a gas if you haven't had a chick slidin' up and down on a slick gas tank with her rose wrapped around you. Her legs wrapped around you with her feet pushing the pinion pad on the back fender, and her hands on your back with thumbs kind a like underneath your armpits so they can pull that rose down on you with some gusto. The feet on the pinion pad is to help push her back up on the tank so she can get a good down stroke. You got to be riding down the road so the vibration of the bike can vibrate the man in the boat.

Now, like I said, in so many words, is there any other way to ride? Hair blowing in the wind with the sweet smell of rose. This does take some practice. A beginner chick is rough, but it's still the only way to go, and girls like to ride on the back. The vibration talks to the guy sailing the boat and you've made your chore a lot easier. So fellows take your lady for a ride. What's under a lady's dress is the same thing that's under a tramp's dress, and they all like to ride.

Sammy Let's Ride

WELL IT'S ABOUT 6 P.M., maybe a little later in the evening, and there's not much traffic on the road. This day it's Sammy, "The Reverend Sammy C." Calvin, one of my main partners outside of the band, along with Tony Townsen and Reese Hawkins, and we leave the big house headed towards Bowlin'brook on Vineville Avenue. Bowlin'brook is west of Macon, and as we leave we start out just riding, not fast, taking it easy. Sammy is on his Triumph, a Tiger 500 that is sweet and not stock. The Rev sits low in the saddle, and I'm on the Green Weenie.

The slow speed doesn't last too long. We increase speed a little and run a little ways, then increase the speed a little more. We do this about four or five times, and we're hauling ass. By the time we get out by the Macon Little Theater we're running about 100 miles per hour. They could hear us back at the Big House, and said they could hear us increase speed each time.

In the area of the theater in the road starts a downgrade. Sammy is on my left as the Rev and me start down the grade, and there is Officer Bedgood. Well Bedgood, who I'll say right now is a damn good man, a man of his word, has this car pulled over. His motorcycle is parked behind the car, and he's standing by the driver's window talking to the driver. He said later that he could hear us coming for five minutes.

Well, as we see him, he sees us. The Rev and myself are in sync when it comes to running, and now we have no choice. No cars on the road, and we have to run for it. Like I said the Rev is on my left, so I have to wait for him to open up the throttle before I can. You see Bedgood has stepped out in the road with helmet in hand to stop us. Sammy skeets by him, but like I said, I couldn't open her up till Sammy got in front of me so I could fall behind him.

I'm about five yards behind Sammy when he goes by Bedgood. Then when I go by he tries to knock me off by swinging his helmet at my head. I do the pony express thing and lean over to the left like I'm going to scoop something off the road. As soon as I get by him I sit straight up and look right back at him. He sees my face real good and knows it's me, plus I've got a bright green bike. Well me and Sammy with our hair blowing in the wind, get away clean. Bedgood knew he couldn't catch us. Sammy and me hid out for about an hour at Phyllis' apartment, that's Sammy's lady who was a super fox, then we head out to party for the night.

Back at the Big House they had a police scanner and heard Bedgood say, "That Allman boy Red Dog and his friend Tuffy just went by me at about 120 miles an hour." Bedgood thought it was Tuffy because Sammy and Tuffy both had black bikes. Well they were about to shit at the house 'cause Sammy and me don't show up for a couple of hours. They don't know if they caught us or not, but they know the police are looking.

Well, I lay dead and hide out around town for a couple of days until I figure it's okay. Then I get on my bike and head to the Sunshine Club, a hole in the wall beer joint where we hung out during our riding days, you could go in this place and talk about anything and it never left the place — a gangster hang out. Of course this place didn't last but a few years.

I didn't know it, but just as I pull up to the Shine, Bedgood pulled in right behind me. He had been laying for me and I never knew he was following me. As I pull up with my bike still running, I'm saying something to Tony, and hear this voice behind me, "Turn off your engine." Then in a southern drawl voice, "Put your kick stand down, Red Dog," and I shit. Like being ambushed in Nam, you got to be calm, so I do as he says and get off my bike.

He says, "That was you and Tuffy that went by me over a hundred the other day."

I said, "I don't know what you are talking about. That was not me."

Then Bedgood says, "Bullshit Red Dog. I know that was you."

I said, "No, it wasn't."

Then he says, if I lie to him he's going to lock my ass up, so I look him straight in the eye and say, "That was not," and he put me in the car, "You are going to jail."

About that time a good size crowd has gathered because they got that Allman boy Red Dog. Tony pulled Bedgood off to the side, Sammy eased up to them and they all talked. Then Bedgood comes over to the police car and lets me out saying, "Red Dog I'm going to ask you one more time, was that you and Tuffy? If you tell me the truth, I'll let you get on your motor and ride out of here. If you lie to me then I'm going to lock your ass under the jail."

With this I'm looking Bedgood dead in the eye to see if he's telling the truth. I figured what the hell, it's a 50-50 chance he'll let me go if I tell him the truth, but if I say no, then I'm surely going to jail.

Well I tell him, "Yes, Bedgood, that was me. I'm not going to tell you who was with me, but I will tell you that it was not Tuffy, and that's the truth."

Bedgood said, "Okay, Red Dog you can get on your bike and ride out of here."

I said, "Thanks," and we all stood there shootin' the shit.

I think the good spirit of Duane was close at hand, and I knew Berry would be relieved to know the situation was over. He just loved me and was worried.

Then I looked over at Tony, Tuffy and Sammy, the four of us rode a hell of a lot together, and I said, "Let's ride."

We used to haul ass on the back roads when we were out T. T. riding, that's Tavern to Tavern, all the way around Macon. This was almost a daily ritual if we're home. We'd do about 70 or so, and make these formations, diamond shapes, wedges, Vs, and stuff like that. With the movement of a finger we would change formations.

To give you an example, just say we are riding, I would take the index finger on my right hand and move it straight and then back down. All this meant was for the guy behind me to pull up alongside. We had all kinds of little signals that could change a formation. If we were in a diamond shape with Tony in the front, Sammy and me behind him, Tuffy behind us and still right in line with Tony, that makes a diamond.

The trick when you are running about 70 on the back roads that are hilly and curvy is to pull in real tight, like a gnat's ass over a rain barrel. Tuffy would pull right up behind Tony with his front wheel about two feet from Tony's back wheel, and straight behind it. Sammy and myself would pull in to where our foot pegs were about three feet apart, and right in the middle of Tony and Tuffy's wheels. You see, that's tight, and you had to listen to the sound of the engines. When you go into a curve you make your adjustment in speed so you didn't lose space. Sammy and me had to change speed a lot because we were on the sides. Try this when you been out riding and drinking all day, and add to it Tuffy and me were heroin addicts.

I'm glad that isn't part of my life anymore. I have no fear of doing it again. You could put it on the table right in front of me and I wouldn't want it. Life passes you by and you don't even know it. Thank God, I'm a survivor. You have to be strong. I just don't like the shit, or alcohol anymore. History.

Boola's Bike Shop

"GET RID OF THE shit!" That was the cry when Duane, Gregg, Kim, Berry, Mike and some biker friends of ours, that's Tuffy, Reverend Samuel C., Ronnie Davis who we called Boola, and Johnny B. Cochran, saw the motorcycle cop pull up on the sidewalk in front of Boola's Bike Shop. Bodies were going assholes and elbows in all directions, until they realized I was on the back of the cop's bike.

I had just wrecked my bike when this older black lady, and her husband who was riding shotgun, ran a stop sign. I had to lay the bike down on her side and let her go. I watched her bounce off the side of the car as I baseball slid on my ass. It shook my tree a little, but I wasn't hurt.

The lady tried to say it was my fault, so I said, "Look. I don't want to hear it. You've torn up my bike. Please just get in your car and leave."

I didn't have any dope on me, I just didn't want her to get in trouble. She tried to rebut until her husband realized what I said. He told her, "Shut up and let's go. It's your fault and the man is letting you go."

Right after they left a motorcycle policeman pulled up. I couldn't get my bike started, so he gave me a ride on the back of his bike up the street about a mile to the shop. I told him what happened, that I told her to leave, so I did a good deed and got a good deed in return. But, everyone was shittin' their pants in the shop for just a few seconds. Kim and Berry were already in the bathroom ready to flush the shit. Now that's moving!

I went in the shop laughing like hell and the officer comes in. Boola met him at the door, and I told him what happened.

The officer rode Boola back to my bike on the back of his, and Boola got her running and back to the shop.

Now she had some damage, so it's bike repair time. Break out the shit because you have to get a buzz and hang out to get your bike fixed. The funny thing is they had just got the shit, so now everybody was cracking up about what happened and Payne said his nuts were dragging on the floor. By now things have cooled out, so we get high, start working on the bikes, shootin' the shit and tellin' stories — just like the one I'm going to lay on you now.

Stay Out of Jail

ONE TIME WE WERE just outside of Hefner, Alabama, coming from Atlanta. I was driving the Winny and we passed two police in a car sitting on the side of the road. I wasn't breaking the law, but I knew by the way they looked at me they were going to put the blue the light special on us. Which they did.

One officer came on to the Winny. Gregg had half a pint of Scotch that was open, but still full, so they made Willie, Gregg and myself get out of the Winny and put us in the back seat of the police car. Willie because he was the road manager, and had the briefcase with the money, Gregg because the Scotch was his, and me because I was driving. Now the scam starts, first they say, "You can't have an open bottle in the camper," but this was b.s., because you could. It was a motor home, not a car, and as long as the driver wasn't drinking it was okay, but we didn't say anything. Then they put a shoebox full of all kinds of drug accessories in between them. The driver pulled out a big "horse" syringe. He worked the plunger in and out saying, "You know the judge don't like long hairs. He likes to put them in jail."

Understanding the situation immediately, I suss out the pinch is coming. Without hesitation I replied, "How much is it going to cost us to stay out of jail."

He said something like, "About $170."

Then I said to Willie, "You got $170?"

Willie said, "Yes," so I said, "Pay the man," and away we went. Assholes.

New Orleans 1970

JUST LIKE THE POLICE in New Orleans when they popped us back in the early '70s after they heard we had a lot of coke. Back at the hotel after the gig, Twiggs and I were just coming out of the elevator on to our floor, the whole band was on the same floor, and then we heard voices and looked to the right. All these guys in beach shirts, shorts, and even business suits came around the corner and down the hall like they were in New Orleans for a convention.

Before we could move they dropped off two at a time in front of our rooms and kicked the doors down. Well hell's bells! I had a chunk of hash in my pocket the size of a golf ball so I pulled it out and dropped it right beside me in to one of those cigarette butt cans with a little hole in the middle of the top. Then Twiggs and I got lucky. The elevator door opened back up, so we stepped backwards right back into it, the door closed and we just looked at each other.

This just gets better now. On the way down to the lobby Twiggs tells me, "Red Dog, you take that entrance to the hotel, and I'll take this entrance so we can see who's getting busted. When we got downstairs two more officers figured out we were with the band, and they take us back upstairs.

Now Tuffy, Mike and Kim were in a room down the hall and around the corner with a couple of guys we knew. They had a nice stash of close to a pound of coke, if you want to call that a "stash," which we just fell into by accident that night. Or, were we set up like our West Coast Brothers, the Grateful Dead? Doesn't it seem odd that the two wildest bands in the country got popped back to back in New Orleans? Well it does to me. Anyway, Tuffy also had three or four Colt .44 cap and ball pistols in the room with him, but for some reason the cops didn't even go to this room.

Back around the corner shit was hittin' the fan. They slapped Betts a few times after they kicked his door down and he put up a fight. When I got there, they had Dickey in his bathroom with a gangbuster hold on him. I was right by the doorway to the bathroom, with this little walk in closet to my right, and said, "What is happening? You can't do that."

Then one officer told them to get me out of there. Well, I grabbed the big round rod you hang your clothes on and say, "I'm not leaving. Why do you want me to leave? So you can beat the shit out of him?" That's when one of the other officers grabbed me by my throat and started choking until I started to pass out. They drug me out of the room, and I think they hit Dickey a couple more times, and Betts went to jail. I think they arrested Gregg, Buffalo, and Jaimoe as well.

Now Jaimoe likes to be freaky. Sometimes he does things other people don't do just to be different and to keep his individuality. When they kicked his door down he was wearing a moo-moo dress type thing, or something real freaky. Well, they thought they had some cross dresser, but boy were they wrong, and off goes Jaimoe with Gregg and Dickey to jail.

Willie went down to get everybody out, but it took hours because it was early Sunday morning. Later in the afternoon Dickey and Gregg sat in with some local bands, and played for free in the park. In those days, you could do outside gigs for free. The People's Music. Now you have to have $1 million worth of insurance. Which seems to me like just another way to keep the people from gathering.

The next day everyone had gone home, but I decided to stay. I asked Mike to tell my wife Miss Bunkie, that I was upset and was going to hang for a few days. We had only been married for a short time and I hadn't settled down yet. That took about a year, but I did stop running around on her.

Right now I was with Lisa Cooper, who was unreal, and to be so young. She was 14 when I met her, but of course I thought she was older. Her and her friends looked like they were 18 and I just never thought to ask.

Payne and me were rooming together. I think it was 1970, and we just got in from a gig at the Warehouse, but didn't see any ladies so we went to Duane and Berry's room. They had a couple of ladies, so we asked them, "You got any friends?"

The girl with Duane said two of her friends just left because everybody had a lady.

I said, "Call them and tell them to come back."

When she did, they said they would be right there, so Kim and I went back to our room. Well, Lisa and Tina came to our room and sat at the foot of my bed. Lisa asked what sign I was, and I told her Aries. Then she asked Payne, and he said he was a Scorpio. Tina jumped in bed with Payne, and Lisa got under the covers with me. What a lady. She was pretty as can be, and had a fantastic body. Plus she knew how to use it. She was my lady, and I was crazy about her. She loved me, but we both knew the time wasn't right. I spent a lot of time with her, and she was the only lady I ever flew to gigs to meet me on the road — that is, the only one who was not my wife.

I spent three days in New Orleans. Three great days. I must say Miss Bunkie was a little upset, and she didn't know about Lisa. At least that's what I thought until I found out later she did, so I promised not to see her again.

But, I did when we went to California to play some gigs in 1976. At the time Lisa lived in San Francisco and came down to Santa Barbara. Well as soon as she showed up, Mike Arts, who was Butch's brother in law and our soundman, his wife, Patty, sees her and called Miss Bunkie. By the time I walked into my room the phone was ringing, and it was Miss Bunkie saying, "She's there, isn't she?"

I said, "Who?"

She said, "You know who the fuck I'm talking about! Lisa Cooper, that's who."

I said, "I haven't seen her. If she was there I didn't know it. I wouldn't mess with her even if she was there."

Well, Lisa was right there on the bed with me, so I told Bunkie goodbye and made love to Lisa, and that was the last time I saw her.

Twiggs Teaches Mr. Smith to Talk

TWIGGS WAS IN A nut house in Buffalo, New York, and we were in a nut house across town. Twiggs was there because of the incident in Buffalo. We were playing this club, and just before the gig, right after dark, I met this lady. We went to an apartment complex within walking distance from the club and sat on a porch of two empty apartments to trade our passions. This night started good but Beelzebub was close at hand.

After the gig the club owner said he wasn't going to pay us. This wasn't the first time this has happened to us, and Twiggs was being real cool. Then the owner said he will pay us. This went back and forth for over an hour, until we went back to the hotel with no money. Now Twiggs was pissed. We needed the $500 to get to Cleveland for the next gig.

The next morning we were going to breakfast and Twiggs stopped me at the door as I was leaving the hotel room. He said, "Augie, the club owner called me and said for me to come to the club. He said he is going to pay us."

I don't know how many times the owner said he will pay then said he wouldn't, but Twiggs said to me, "If he don't pay us I'm going to kill him. I'll stab him with my knife."

I said, "Twiggs, don't talk that shit," and he said, "Just make sure I get my camera." Twiggs took most of the pictures of the band during those days.

I said, "O.K. but don't do that." Now, I know Twiggs, if he said he was going to do something then that's what he did, but this time I thought he was just mad. I went on with Duane, Berry, and I believe Gregg and Jaimoe to breakfast. We got back from eating and Butch opened the door to the room and says, "Twiggs has killed the club owner." When

Twiggs got to the club the owner said he wasn't going to pay, and Twiggs went over the bar and stabbed him.

Shit has now hit the fan. In mass confusion we got everything together and left for Cleveland leaving Twiggs behind, which was killing me because I didn't want to leave him. I had a crazy thought of gangbustering the jail and getting him out, but I knew I couldn't do that. I'm still left with the pain of leaving him behind. To understand my feeling of leaving him you need to read the book The Frozen Chosin, which is about the great Marine Corp. General Chesty Puller at the battle of Changjin Reservoir during the Korean Conflict.

During our gig in Cleveland the music was high but the moral was low. We got our first taste of playing to a missing spirit. Afterwards we headed back home to Macon. Twiggs ended up spending six months in the county jail, and a year in the nut house. He did a bad thing, but the club owner asked for it. Now that doesn't make it right, but what can I say, put your finger under the falling blade and you lose it.

During the time Twiggs was in the nut house we worked our asses off to pay his legal fees, which weren't cheap. I think we did 278 one-nighters that year. We hold the record for that. The group Chicago Transit Authority came close, but they used two complete sets of equipment and two road crews. They would leap frog. One crew did one show, and the second crew did the next. We just packed her up and knocked 'em out. Two hundred and seventy eight bad ones with three roadies and one road manager. That's probably one of the major reasons we did a lot of drugs. We had to keep going. We needed something to keep us up and something to put us to sleep.

Well about two weeks before Brother Duane's passing, Berry, Kim, Duane and myself went to a nut house in Buffalo to clean out. Our place was different than the one Twiggs was in. His was a big building and run by the state. Ours was an old two- or three-story house converted to a private little nut house. They didn't even have the word rehab at this time.

I didn't really even need to go. I stopped using six days before we left for Buffalo, and the worst part was over for me. But Duane was going, and where Duane went I went. He told me I was going with him. He kept his dog with him all the time.

While we were cleaning out I met a patient, this fox and a real fine girl. The first day I talked to her, and things went real well. We arranged to meet that night so we could do Red Dog things, but she didn't show up. When I saw her the next day it was like I was talking to a stranger, so I laid the groundwork again, and again she didn't show. Shit. I said, "What the fuck is happening?" This happened a few times until another patient I was talking with finally told me they hit her with shock treatment everyday. Damn! No wonder we couldn't meet for Red Dog things. I get in her head in the morning, and they burn me out in the afternoon. I don't care what anybody says, shock treatment is bull.

About the third day Big Linda and Berry's sister, Candy who was now doing a thing with Kim, came to visit. They stayed at a hotel not far from where we were. One night Berry and Kim slipped out to be with their ladies and get some beer. We were still on Methadone too, so they got a good buzz that night. Duane wasn't overjoyed when the doctor said something to him about it. He didn't raise hell with Kim and Berry. He just said it wasn't cool. Berry said, "You're right. That was a bad move," but Kim was ready to go again.

The next day Duane and I were going to see Twiggs for the first time since the incident, but I ended up going by myself, because Duane didn't want Twiggs to see him like that. I don't think he really wanted to see Twiggs in that environment either. It would have hurt him to see Twiggs like that, then have to leave him there.

Anyway, they took me to see Twiggs, who is supposed to be a nut in another nut house. They put me in the back of a car with no inside door handles and a wire cage that separated the front from the back. I thought it was pretty strange because I was there to clean out, and they acted like I was dangerous.

When I was visiting with Twiggs, he could tell I was upset. Tears came down my cheeks as soon as my eyes touched his, so he just patted me on the back and said, "It's okay Augie, I'm doing fine." Then he told me a story.

After about two months of him being there he heard that another patient, Mr. Smith, had not spoken a word in around 25 years. This became a challenge to Twiggs. If he could get Mr. Smith to talk that would be great, and something no one else could do, so Twiggs started stopping by Mr. Smith's room.

Mr. Smith wouldn't say a word no matter what Twiggy said or did, until one day when the light went on. He noticed Mr. Smith always read. He mostly read about the civil war, and this was right up brother Twiggs's alley. Being that he was originally from Macon he knew some things about the Civil War.

One day Twiggs went into Mr. Smith's room and told him that he can't read, but he has a book on the civil war and wants to learn about it. He wondered if Mr. Smith would teach him to read. This went on for about a week until finally Mr. Smith spoke to Twiggs and started teaching Twiggs to read. Twiggs said nothing to anyone. Mr. Smith would only talk to him, and that was only if they were alone. That's until one day when Twiggs told Mr. Smith, "Wouldn't it be great if when Dr. Jones comes in the morning you said hi to him."

For 25 years Dr. Jones had entered the hospital, the nut house, and spoke to patients in the big lounge near the front of the building. He would say good morning to different patients, and they would say something back to him, but not Mr. Smith.

The next morning Dr. Jones came in and did his thing. He walked a straight line in from the front door to his office. Walked straight ahead and without looking said, "Good morning, Mr. Smith." To which Mr. Smith said, "Good morning, Dr. Jones."

Now without loosing his stride he did a column right, walked right up to Mr. Smith, and said, "May I see you in my office for a moment, Mr. Smith?"

Mr. Smith said, "Yes, sir," and away they went.

Twiggs had done a great thing, and he did things like this all the time. Like getting Mr. Smith to talk.

The next day after seeing Twiggs we left our nut house and headed home. That morning Duane looked over and I was sitting up in bed nodded out, in and out from the Methadone treatments, so when the doctor came in Duane went ballistic on him. I never saw him do that except when he got on me for smoking hash on the plane, and that wasn't close to this.

He started hollering at the doctor, looking at him and pointing to me, "Look at him. You got him all fucked up again, and he was straight when we got here. He had already cleaned up, and you got him all fucked up again. We are leaving. We are getting out of here." And that's what we did. Duane took us right out of there and home.

A couple of days later Beelzebub was back knocking at our door. Big Bro was gone, and slowly, very slowly, we started to fall apart.

Crab Free and Happy

THE CRABS, THOSE LITTLE creatures that crawl and bite, and make you scratch your ass off, showed up one day in the summer of 1970 when we were on our way through Texas.

We stopped in Amarillo to de-crab. We got one room for the ten of us. Twiggs told the motel people we just wanted to shower and we would be gone, and that's why we just needed one room. He told them they could rent the room again after we left.

We had already got about eight bottles of A-200, and boy did they look at Twiggs at the drug store when he asked for eight bottles of that. Twiggs just smiled and said, "Have a good life."

He used to say the same thing when we went through tollbooths and the attendant said something smart-ass like, "You girls have a nice trip." Twiggs would smile and say as we pulled away, "Have a good life."

After we got the room me and Twiggs took all of our clothes, and all of the linen and everything from the Winnebago, to the wash and fold laundry mat. Then we took the Winny to a wash house and told them to use a lot of disinfectant on her.

Twiggs and me grabbed a cab back to the hotel so we could start de-crabbing along with everyone else. You could smell the A-200 across the street. When the maid brought us more towels, I don't think she could believe what she was seeing and smelling. Here were ten men sitting around the room naked and smelling like A-200. You know what that shit smells like. Well, we finished up and cuffed on down the road. Crab free and happy.

The Second Atlanta Pop Festival

I won't ever forget the second Atlanta Pop Festival. It was twenty miles from the house down in Byron, Georgia. The country folks around couldn't believe what they were seeing. Hippies everywhere, camped in people's yards, smoking pot, taking acid, and running around naked jumping off of bridges into creeks. I don't think the police much enjoyed seeing the guys running and swimming naked, but they sure liked the girls doing it.

Payne rode out to the site on his 350 Honda, and Callahan rode with me in the Winny. We parked her backstage in the camper area, put the canvas roof up, and made a patio on the side. Then we went around and checked things out. Within two minutes we had more girls than we could handle. After spending the day romping, we jumped on Payne's 350 Honda and rode home. That's right, there was three of us on that one small bike for 20 miles down the interstate.

I remember the night we played too. Wow! Fuckin' wow! It was about 30 minutes before sunset, and there were thousands and thousands of people inside the fenced area, and even more on the other side that didn't pay. When the announcer said, "The Allman Brothers Band," people on the outside decided to come in because they had to see the Brothers, so that's what they did. The fences came down like they weren't even there, and they saw the Brothers kick ass. Every gig we did just seemed to be getting better, and this was one of the best ever. It was our backyard, this was the original Allman Brothers Band, and we were there to spread our religion. After the set, you knew you had been to church.

We played during the transition of daylight to darkness, which was the best time at an outdoor event where people were tripping. I had made some Red Dog potion, and a lot of people back stage were in the same condition as a lot of the people out front.

We were waiting for Jimi Hendrix to go on after we played, and packed the gear in the truck. Still waiting on Jimi this girl I know goes off. I mean she went off. She was running around screaming at the top of her voice, "Red Dog of The Allman Brothers, I love you." Then right behind it she hollered, "Red Dog of the Allman Brothers, I hate you." She hollered out those two things about a hundred times, so I went and I hid. Everybody there knew who Red Dog was, and I was tripping, but I knew not to go near her. I was laying low. Real low.

Hendrix finally came on and played one hell of a set, but the night belonged to the Allman Brothers.

Jacksonville Freak Off

IT WAS A FEW years after that when I saw my crazy lady friend from the Atlanta Pop Festival again. When I did, we call this the Jacksonville freak-off, she showed up at a gig in Jacksonville, Florida with five other lady friends. We were glad to have them, so we went to the hotel and partied up.

This was a true freak-off, with naked bodies everywhere. Kim had just come in the room and saw my legs sticking out one end of the covers, and saw Larry Howard's head sticking out the other end. He said, "The dog has come out," because it looked like Larry and I were going at it until somebody pulled the covers back, and there she was between us.

Payne about fell out laughing, and said, "I couldn't see her under the covers. I thought you were doing Howard." Boy, am I glad she was there.

Now Twiggs is the master of freak-offs and Payne, Mike, Joe Dan, Larry, Howard, and myself can lay them down. But these ladies could go. I mean wow! That's all except the one who sat in the chair with her clothes on and just watched. By daylight there's not a pole standing in the house, and we shifted to plan B. Break out the tools and let it eat, which we did. Now I can't go into details, but believe me this was the Jacksonville freak-off roadie style.

Brother R.C.

Speaking of Jacksonville reminds me of the time in the beginning of 1971. We were playing at the Coliseum over by the Gator Bowl, and had just loaded in. It was about two in the afternoon when Callahan was moving the truck and hit a car right by the loading ramp.

Long hairs weren't accepted at the time. The police were already there, and they were watching him to begin with, so they saw him do it; this wild looking maniac guy who was all messed up and had alcohol on his breath. They were lying dead for him, and bang, he gave them just what they wanted. Now he was in the police car getting ready to go to jail.

Well just before they drove off my brother R.C., who was on the Jacksonville Police Department, drove up in his police car and got out. I told him what happened, and he went over and talked to the other policeman, and they let Mike go without even a ticket. Thank you R.C. and your fellow policeman.

The next morning my brother came by our hotel room in his uniform to say good bye. He knocked on the room door, and a friend of ours, who was in the room dealing us some goodies went to the door and looked out the peephole, "It's the cops."

Everyone inside started getting in gear, and getting it together, sitting on the toilet in stand by mode. I realized it might be my brother, so I run over and look through the peephole. Well, it was R.C., so I opened the door and there was his big badge staring everyone in the face. Panic! Heart in your ass time, until I quickly turned and said it was my brother. Everything almost got flushed down the toilet, but not yet. We all laugh like hell, and I talked with my brother for a while. We still laugh about it today.

Angel Dust to Layla

I CAN'T REMEMBER WHERE the hell we were coming from, but we were somewhere up around Washington D.C., at this theater in the round; a stage in the middle with seats all around.

We were traveling in the Winnebago, and when we got to the theater and have to wait a while so the building crew can finish up a few things. While we are waiting the promoter's staff said, "They have some great smoke, but to be careful." Well, you know how it is when you've been out of smoke all day and can't wait to put your lips on a fat joint? And these people are saying be careful? Shit man, let me at it.

We're all sitting in a circle, B.O., Kim, Mike, Me, Gregg, Butch, some of the promoter's staff and maybe one or two more of my brothers. We started smoking this joint and they say take it easy. Shit, I'm tokin' up, sucking in big-ass hits. Well kiss my ass I can't move. I mean I can't move. Not even a friggin' finger. I start to think I'm going crazy. Now I find out later that this shit is Angel Dust. Do I need to say more? I think B.O. and Butch notice something's up and one of them said, "Come on Red Dog, lets go to the Winnebago."

I could not respond. I couldn't get up. I just sat there looking straight ahead thinking, I'm going nuts and I will never be right again. Well, by me not moving at all they reached down and helped me up. With one on each side of me, we walked to the Winnebago. When we get there I'm thinking; I'll see Duane, we will talk, and it will be all right. Well right on, the first person I see is Duane. Yeah, we're going to be okay. Duane takes one look at me and says, "You been smoking that shit? That shit will make you go crazy."

In my mind I'm thinking string me up momma, send out the SOS, I'm history. I know I've gone crazy now. They put me in the bottom bed in the back lounge, and after a while Jaimoe came back. He was sitting with me talking. You know how you just sit with someone that's out there and talk them back down? Well all of the sudden I grabbed him by the arm and say, "Jaimoe I got it all figured out. We've done turned this bad boy, the Winnebago, over and we've been dead for three or four days."

Well, shit. Kiss Jaimoe goodbye. Those words came out of my mouth and Jaimoe was up and gone. I know he must have been thinking, "I got to leave that one with you Augie."

How I can remember this much is beyond me, so the last piece of this trip is what I was told. We pulled into a station after the show to get gas, so I got out and was pissing on the gas pump. Just standing there with my rosy pink, baby lookin' pretty pole in my hand, pissing on the pump. Yes sir, right in front of God and everybody.

Well, Duane and Berry told me to go to the bathroom and pee, but I quickly respond, "I'm in the friggin bathroom." With that said, they just let me finish and I got back on the Winny to sleep off this friggin' nightmare. It was nice to wake up the next morning and find that somebody had put the world back together again. Never again will I say, "If you can smoke it, I can handle it." I learned that the hard way. No more angel dust. I can smell that shit, not even lit, a mile away.

Now somewhere back at the gig Butchy, who was playing our road manager after the Twiggs thing in Buffalo, and before we got Willie "the four speed" Perkins, picked up the money from the gig, and had it in a brown paper bag. While relieving himself he put the bag on top of the urinal then walked out and left it there.

Well thank the spirits Berry walked in just behind Butchy leaving. Berry evidently used the same pisser and sees this bag. Well what the hell is this? No shit! A bag full of money. Goddamn we hit the jackpot! This is what B.O., thinks right? You know what I'm saying, you find a bag of money and you go ape. It's everybody's dream to find a bag of money.

With the bag tucked up under his shirt, B.O. heads for the Winny. He gets there and is telling everyone, look what I found. He's laughing and carrying on, and he went to the back of the Winny to count the money when Butch walks in with his face blank. They say he looked like he had died. He had already been back to the bathroom and the money was gone. He didn't know Berry went in after he left, and now he has to tell us all that he, Mr. Super Brain, has lost the money. Yep, the smart one has done it. He started to tell us, and everyone realized that the money in the brown bag Berry had was the same brown bag that Butchy lost. There were some good spirits watching over us that day. All the way around. You know what I mean?

When Callahan and me got to Atlanta around 4 in the afternoon I was ready to party again. I found some good smoke and took a nice mellow hit of acid. No angel dust! Hell, Callahan was going around trying to sell or trade the shit because Duane said to get rid of it. And that's what we did, what he didn't sell or trade we threw away. That is all except for the bag Callahan stashed. I don't think Duane ever knew he held back a bag. If he did, he never said anything. I think Mike, Gregg, and Kim kept that pretty well hidden.

Duane wouldn't tell you to do something if he didn't mean it. He didn't have to speak twice. He was the leader. He was, and no disrespect intended, like our Jesus Christ. We followed him and his word. You might say the rest of the band went along and preached with him. How lucky we were to have six great preachers in one church with four pulpit sitters. Maybe one acid trip too many; acid trip #578 as I laugh, but you know what I mean.

Of course sometimes we might try to slip one by him. Like the time Big Brother said, no more smoking on the planes. We used to go in the bathroom and smoke reefer. And hell, you could smell the shit all over the plane. So Big Brother said no more smoking on the planes.

Two days later we were flying from San Diego to L.A. I'm tripping on mushrooms and Gregg comes back from the bathroom, hands me the hash, and the hash pipe that Kim had given him. You see where I'm going? Well naturally Duane caught me holding the hash and the pipe. He went to hollering and everyone on the plane could hear him, "I said not to smoke that shit on the planes. Do you want to get us busted?"

Now I ain't smoked shit. I was just handed the pipe in case I wanted to do it. It's one of the times you want to hit the friggin' guy, but you love him too much so you just let your eyes flood up and flow. Well, two minutes later he's putting his arm around me and tells me he's sorry, but if he says don't do something don't do it. That was the only time Duane ever raised his voice to me. He never had to again. See, I believe if a person is your friend and he's in charge, you should never put yourself in a situation where your friend has to say something negative to you. You're his friend and that makes it hard enough for him to say something. So as a friend, don't make them feel uncomfortable. Dig?

The next day the band flew from Charlotte to Miami. Callahan drove the equipment truck and I drove the Winny from Atlanta. We took off around seven o'clock at night, and headed for Miami down good ol' Interstate 75. We sure as hell burnt that road up in those days. Mike had this honey with him in the little cab of the truck, but I had the deal. The whole friggin' Winnebago to myself and this sweet little blonde with a small waist, a big crapamay that she kept up in the air while stroking her lollipop all the way to Miami. Of course, we had to stop on numerous occasions for a little rose. All those beds on the Winny, we had to try them out. Like I didn't already know. It took me and Callahan three days to get from Charlotte to Miami, with a stop in Atlanta where we picked up the ladies and a quick stop in Macon. Then of course there were the stops to get the roses.

We got to Miami around 6:00 in the morning, joined the band and got cleaned up. We had a gig that night, and played on one of those roll-up stages. It was in a small park, like a long narrow lot in between the streets. I think some local bands were playing there also.

Tom Dowd, who was our producer and also Eric Clapton's, brought the Layla band to the gig and introduced us to them afterwards because Eric wanted to meet Duane. Duane and Eric rapped, and the next thing I knew we were at Criteria Recording Studios. Eric was recording the Layla album and he wanted Duane to play on it. That's because he was the only guitar player he heard that he could trust, and he wanted to concentrate on his singing. So you can see how it all came about, and folks that's history. I think we were in Studio B, I was sitting in the control room looking out into the studio, and there was the Layla band with Duane and Dickey playing. Dickey played for awhile then sat down to listen. I wish he had played longer, but not this time. He chose to listen.

Duane and Eric played a little longer then we left. But what a sight! The only thing I can think of that impressed me like that was when Duane, Dickey, Jerry Garcia, and Bob Weir played together. For sure anytime the Dead and the Brothers played together; well that was just icing on the cake because it would gather in the spirits, past and present.

We only had one gig left after Miami then went home to Macon. Duane went on back to Miami and played on the now famous Layla album. When Clapton went on the road Duane did two gigs with them, one in Tampa and one in Syracuse, then he came back home. "They can play, but not like us, " he told me. "I had to come home so I could get off," meaning play music with his brothers. Duane told me more than once it's the only band that gets him off, and I'm sure it's the same with my other brothers.

I've said it 100 times, there's nothing like Allman Brothers' music. Then and now. I've heard it so many ways. Berry and Jaimoe, and any combination of players from the band you could imagine, sitting in the music room in the Big House at three in the morning playing their asses off. Making up shit as they go and free style jamming, or maybe working on something. Time had no limit and every night was different. Different brothers jamming together making great music, of which 99 percent has never been heard but by only a few sets of ears.

Wow! What a way to make a living. Joe Dan, Mike, Kim, and myself would work on equipment while listening to ass kicking music. Of course we kept a buzz and threw a little rose in on the side. What more could you ask for? We had a house full of love. Brothers, the road goes on forever. Look at us. What's left? Gregg, Butch, Jaimoe, and me — Red Dog — semper fi, always faithful, and Brother Dickey who's on leave of absence.

If you think Gregg, Butch, Jaimoe and Dickey can't do a concert without a bass player, let me tell you something; think again! I guarantee you the four of them could give you a show you would never forget. I would personally love to hear it. That would be nice to listen to the four of them play off each other. The root system. The tree might have lost a few branches, but we still have the roots.

So you see, you can put anybody else up there with my brothers, but if you do get up there to jam with them you better come to play, because you have to hold your own with this band. And that's the way it will be, until one by one we rendezvous with our brothers who are a little further on up the road. It reminds me of a song I wrote not long after the passing of Brother Twiggs. Sometimes it's hard to write this because I do miss my brothers.

"I Hate To Say So Long"

Three of my brothers
They are gone Three
of my brothers I hate
to say so long

You have to understand The
relationship at hand Aaaahhh,
I hate to say so long

Brother Twiggs
He taught me everything I know
To value my mind
To treat it like gold

Brother Berry
We used to trade lines
While sipping wine with the ladies
And talk about the days of sailing on the seas
And my Brother Duane, the King

He taught me to be honest and true
And to stand by my convictions
They will always see me through

Ah I hate to say so long

Three of my brothers
They are gone

Three of my Brothers
I hate to say so long

(Talk this part in my low preacher's voice)

Yes I do lord
Yes I do
Since they've gone,
The days are cold,
And the nights are long

Lord, Lord I don't know what to say,
Since you took them away Three of
my Brothers
They are gone Three
of my Brothers I hate
to say so long

    This still brings tears to my eyes, but that's me, hard on the outside and soft in. I will say I'm only hard when I think I have to be. I don't care what they say, you can only turn a cheek so much and one has to stand up for himself. Remember, in this world kindness is mistaken for weakness. So once in awhile you have to bark, but hopefully not too loud.

Wreckin' the Winny

WHILE I WAS WRITING the song about Brother Twiggs I could see him leaning out the window of our hotel room, but I'm not going to say where. He was hollering, "Red Dog! Red Dog! Nooo ... Nooo," but I couldn't hear him as I was driving the Winny out of the parking lot behind the hotel.

The noise of the engine drowned out voices, plus he was up on the 22nd floor. I was laughing because he looked so funny, and I thought, "He's just playing with me." But you see he's way up and could see the parking lot really well from where he was. You know, he had a bird's eye view. He could see I'm cutting the corner too sharp, and getting ready to run right over top of this Volkswagen Beetle Bug. Which I did while I was looking up and laughing at Twiggs. Oh shit! I flattened that friggin' bug like it wasn't there, but I was high on Duji, heroin, so my nervous system was calm, and I just kept right on driving out of the parking lot like nothing ever happened.

Twiggs on the other end has just shit all over himself. He sees lawsuit and all, and me going to jail. In his mind we were screwed, but have no fear the good spirit of the hound is near. I just moved right out of there, took care of business, and parked the Winny about 40 blocks away; never to see that parking lot again. Can you believe nobody saw that?

I never heard about it except from Twiggs. I got harassed and laughed at a lot by the band, and I was sorry for running over that little bug, but sometimes instinct takes over and you just do what you have to do. I had to ditch out, split, duff. You know, leave on the run.

Three Alabama Ladies

I HAVE TO MENTION the Alabama ladies, the three ladies with hearts the size of the earth. We met for the first time in Nashville about 1970, but we didn't have much to do with them at the gig. We were staying at the Holiday Inn out by the airport where there was nothing around for miles, except airport and motel. Nothing was open, so we couldn't get any food. Plus nobody had any rose. Nobody.

I was messed up and hungry as hell, so I'm sittin' on the floor in the hallway eating crackers off of a tray that was ready to go back to the kitchen. I was eating away and drinking the water when the night watchman came by, so I pulled a B.O., on him and started grabbing food off the plate and putting it in my mouth. He didn't know what to do. Right in front of him was this longhair freak, eating food with his hands like a wild man. He may have had a flash, like, I better not fuck with the guy, and then he walked off.

After he left, this female head stuck out of a room across the hall and to my right. Hell's bells, this is my lucky night. She told me I better get in there before he comes back. Well, no problem. Rose over food. I was up and in the room. Well, these girls are good size ladies, so I told them, "I'll be right back," and went to my room to think for a minute. Now, there wasn't any rose nowhere around, and nobody would know, so I busted back down to their room. Couldn't turn on the rose for a minute around the Allman Brothers. We could smell its scent for miles.

When I got in the room Mike is there. Now two Allman Brothers and three ladies in a room spells fun time. So we got at it. Pretty soon there was a knock on the door, and Berry came in to see the biggest one laying on her back with my little red head bobbing up and down. You couldn't really see the rest of me too much because I sank down in her. It was like her body wrapped around me, and all you could see was my head going up and down; licking it Red Dog style. Now some people say they didn't show up at their room, but it seems to me I saw everyone ease in and ease out.

The next thing, the three ladies, Mike, Kim, and me all got in their Volkswagen Beetle Bug and went for Krystal Burgers. What a sight. That's how we met the three Alabama ladies. For the first four or five years, they showed up at all of the Allman Brother gigs within 400 miles of Huntsville, and sometimes they would extend their boundaries if the gig was big enough.

Last Run of the Winny

Hell, while I'm at it I may as well tell you about the last run of the Winny. Yes sir, I think that is the fastest we ever got out of town. Once again we were on the run, so once again I'm not going to say where we were, but we were the opening act for a three-band bill. When we finished the roadies had to stay to load out while the band went on to the hotel.

Now, this place had a big parking lot, and the Winny was blocked in, so just before the show ended I'm outside trying to figure out how to get the Winny out of there. Yes, I think I see how I can do it, so I jump in the Winny and start her up. Well, that's right where shit went wrong.

As I started the Winny my right foot got caught on the gas pedal, and the heel of my left foot hung up under the brake pedal. I usually started the Winny fast with one foot on the gas. At the same time, I put her in gear as I would take my foot off the gas and put it on the brake, you know, all in one motion, but doing it so you don't go anywhere. Well, like I said my foot got hung up. The gas pedal was all the way down and no brake. Can't push the brake. My heel was under it.

The Winny leapt forward with great gusto, and smashed right into this van. Hit it dead center on the driver's side and slammed it under a shed full of fifty-gallon drums near the side of the building. Well, with this the roof of the shed fell down on a van, so now this van is fucked up. All over. But that's not the half of it.

At the same time all this was happening I grabbed the gearshift, and threw her up into park thinking, "Shit, I have got to get this bitch stopped." But not yet! She doesn't go into park. The shifter stopped in reverse, and now the Winny is moving the opposite direction with great speed, so I throw my head out the window while I'm trying to get her up into park, and wham! Bam! This brand new car goes flying. How many cars she hit I don't know, but what I do know is the Winny had finally stopped. The engine cut off, so I got out to survey the damage to the Winny and not a dent! The thing was like a tank on the outside.

Well hell, now I have all kinds of room to get out of there. So that's exactly what I did, and once again nobody knew it was me. I headed straight for the hotel like lightning and told Duane what happened. I was telling him what happened, saying we have to get the hell out of there, and without a question, or I should say without a word Duane immediately started knocking on doors, "Get up right now, we have to get the hell out of here." Everyone could tell by the sound of his voice that it wasn't time to talk but to move. You didn't have to think in these situations, you just acted.

A few minutes after I got to the hotel, brothers Kim, Mike, and Joe Dan all showed up at the same time, so we were together, which was good. Time to duff, and we are ready to go, but no Gregg, so Duane goes back into the hotel to get him, and Gregg was getting some rose. So Duane slapped him on the butt and says, "Let's get out of here." Maximus is pissing and moaning, but we were on the run and you do what you have to do — run. So to all the ladies we left behind that night, our most humble apologies, and may the sweet smell of your rose pass our way once again.

We headed for New York City so the band could fly to California. My adrenaline was sky high for about an hour, but while I'm driving the Winny I calmed down and was about to go to sleep. Duane was sitting beside me and I told him, "I'm falling asleep." I said I might have been calm on the outside, but I was freaking on the inside, so Duane said to let him drive, and while we were still moving we switched. He drove the Winny on in to New York, and we stayed at the Holiday Inn until our plane was to leave that afternoon. I was going to drive the Winny on back to Macon, but she wouldn't start. The Winny would run no more.

Duane said, "Good. Have it towed home and get Red Dog a plane ticket to California. I'm tired of driving to gigs. It's time we start flying." Which is exactly what we did. Now I was happy as hell. I didn't want to drive the Winny back to Macon, I wanted to go with the band. All for one and one for all. Hora Semper Fi. The Brotherhood.

Alabama Bust

This story actually starts out in Baton Rouge at the fairgrounds or some place where they hold a rodeo. As my memory serves me, we were not all present at this gig. Willie, Duane, Dickey, Gregg, Butch, Jaimoe, Tuffy, Joe Dan, and me were all there. Mike Callahan was in Tarpon Springs, Florida going to court for a lawsuit, which he won, Kim was in Macon after being shot in the leg by the police, and Twiggs was in jail for the deal in Buffalo.

Before the gig somebody gave me two packs of chocolate Nestlé's Quik mescaline, so I head straight for the dressing room, "Hey, look what I got. Nestlé's Quik chocolate mescaline." Of course everybody says, "Lets see." They all start tasting it and saying, "It does taste like Nestlé's Quik," so we go through one pack, except for Willie, he doesn't trip, and Joe Dan, who doesn't trip since he was tripping and saw God while he was in jail. He thought the turnkey was the keeper of the pearly gates, and kept telling him, "It's okay brother. It's okay my brother." Of course, it was not okay the next morning when he came down and he was in jail. That's why you didn't even walk by J.D. with acid.

Wow what a gig. Did we ever get off. We kicked ass that night. Back then when we tripped the band always played good. Oh, there were mistakes, but you couldn't beat the feel of the gigs. We were all in tune with each other, and the audience — the people, the Mushroom People as I always called them. Wow, you talk about gigs and highs. Nothing on this planet can come close to matching the feeling and intuneness of the Dead Heads and Mushroom People when they come together at a Dead-Brothers concert, or you could say an Allman Brothers-Grateful Dead concert. Who cares what you call it, it was great. Liquid drops on little piles of mushrooms. Hold on to your horses Nelly.

If I'm not mistaken it seems like after that gig in our rush to get to the next one, and get away from the straight working class in the area, I failed to notice one small detail. The sliding door wasn't exactly up high enough for the top of the truck, a straight body Easy Haul, to clear. And I politely knocked the door out of its track on the right side as you exit, and bent the track on the frame of the building. Well, this is just great. The guys who worked there are freaking out. I mean they are losing it. Jumping up and down, screaming and saying who is going to pay for this? Call the police. Everybody's gone home. There ain't no way to tell how much it's going to cost to fix it.

Right away I feel a redneck scam coming on.

"You can't leave," one potbelly fart says, "We called the police and you're going to pay for this."

About the same time Tuffy says, "You got a torch here? You must have a damn torch."

The guy says, "Yes," and Tuffy tells him to get the friggin' thing. So he does, and Tuffy lights the torch. Then he holds the torch up and politely lit his cigar. Well, the guy's eyes just about fell out. Joe Dan and me just laugh. Tuffy straightens out the track with a hammer and the torch just as the police are pulling up. Now remember we are raging on good Nestlé's, (laughing).

Well when the police get there the antennas go out, you know, trying to pick up on all wave links and not wanting to go to jail. But the police were nice this time and said, "Go ahead, you've fixed the door." I told them we wouldn't charge them for fixing the door, and they didn't like this, so we left to join the band at the hotel.

We all left for the next gig after telling about the night's activities. I drove the truck. Dickey and Joe Dan were with me, and everyone else was in two rented cars. Now remember, we only ate one pack of the Quik, so as we headed for the next gig I told Dickey I had another pack. He says, "Let me see it," and here we go again — only this time Dickey and me eat the whole thing.

Now, as long as the truck is moving I'm okay, and everything was great. But when we stopped that was another flea on the dog. When you do something so much it just becomes normal. No white lines trying to leap off the road into the cab of the truck, and no trails from lights, until we pulled into a gas station. I don't even know where, just a gas station that came out of the dark. I pulled up to the gas pump, shut her down, and this guy comes out. Now, when I first looked at him coming out the door he was tall and thin. He looked like one of those backwoods guys that does strange things. As he got in front of the truck I noticed a slight change in his appearance, like skin and flesh melting down his face. He walked on around and up to the driver's window and says, "Can I help you?"

Me being cool, and one must remain calm, as I'm looking at his face and there's no meat on it; just blood running down from where his eyes, ears, nose and mouth was, but no flesh, just bone. I tell myself, "Red Dog, you are just tripping, nothing more. Ain't it fun, look at this shit."

Then I say to the attendant, "Yes sir, fill it up please."

I turned immediately to Dickey, who is sitting in the middle next to Joe Dan, who was riding shotgun, and say, "Did you see what I saw?" His eyes just got big and we moved on. I'm not sure about the rest of the way. All I can remember is taking some reds to come down.

Now my understanding of the situation was; a few hours earlier and somewhere along the way, I had made a wrong turn. After that, I don't know how long after, we switched drivers all the way around. Hell, all I know is I ended up in the backseat of one of the cars.

After the switch, we stopped to eat breakfast at this redneck back-in-the-woods joint. Willie, Duane, Joe Dan, Gregg, Tuffy and Butch all went inside to eat. Dickey is out in the parking lot throwing up from the reds he ate to come down off the Quik. Well the lady that runs the joint can't handle it, and she doesn't want to serve the Hippies — low rent trash. Her husband is the chief of police and tells her to go ahead and feed the hippies. Then, oh shit, piss on the wall, kick the friggin' cat. It happened.

Our beloved brother Jaimoe walked in.

Now, if you don't know about the Allman Brothers, we're all white and Jaimoe is black, so the friggin' lady loses it right there. I mean right there.

"I ain't feeding the nigger," she says.

Of course the nosey fat chief is out sticking his nose where he shouldn't be. He's looking in the cars and he sees my shit in my coat pocket. The next thing I know, I'm waking up with the chief of police's left forearm and the weight of a two hundred pound gorilla across my chest. I can't move. With plastic explosives I couldn't get this fat slob off of me, and with his right hand he reached in and pulled out a vial full of pot and a vial of penicillin. As I see Berry's head pop up from the front seat, and look back at me with eyes big as shit to see what was happening, the cop says, "You and you are under arrest for the possession of marijuana. And what's this?"

I tell him penicillin.

They put Berry and myself in a police car and take us to jail. On the way the chief radios and tells Jethro to go arrest everyone else. Now Jethro, if you can picture this, is just like the guy on the Beverly Hillbillies, so you know we're in shit. Plus somebody threw a bag of heroin out the window as the car leaves the parking lot and some guy sees it and picks it up, but that will surface again later.

Now, we're all in jail. This jail is your typical nine-cell jail. I can't tell you what the front of the building looked like. All I know is it faced the main highway, which was the only road in town, I think. There was a gravel parking lot on one side, and a side door that led from the parking lot into the jail. Now, when you open the door you could see into the first cell on the right. There was no cell on the left as there is a door that leads to the main office, which was the only office I saw.

You could pass the first cell block on the right, which was made up of three cells next to each other, and if you didn't turn left to the office, you went straight for 15 feet. Turn left or right, there are three cells, and I'm in the first cell on the cell block on the back right. As you come in the side door Gregg and Tuffy are in the first cell on the right. Dickey was in the cell next to me and was out of it. How else can you say it, from eating the reds to come down. Did he come down? Way down. He ended up sleeping for two days of the three we were in jail. And Joe Dan ... Ah Shit, who cares where the hell we were in the jail. One thing for sure, we were in jail, but it is important about the first cell on the right that Gregg and Tuffy were in.

Somebody yelled out, "How is Gregg?" I think it was Duane who yelled back, "He's freakin' out," and everyone laughed.

They had taken everyone to the office one at a time for questions and answers, you know, interrogation. I was last, which I thought I would be because I had the pot. First they asked me about the vial of pills, which was penicillin that I needed for the bug I picked up, so I told them I had the clap. Shit, I might as well have said I had the friggin' plague or something. About the same time this guy walks in with the bag of heroin, you know a $10 bag, and gives it to the chief. The chief opened it up, then stuck it under my nose, and said in his funny accent country ass voice, "What is this? Herrin? (Meaning heroin)."

Well, since he put it under my nose I felt, being that he asked me what it was, I would find out for him. I gave a big snort inward through my right nostril and politely said, "It tastes like B.C. to me. You know? The headache powder."

He went to yelling, "He snorted up the evidence! He snorted up the evidence," and he freaked out right there in front of me. I thought he was going to foam at the mouth. He didn't know what to do, so he put me in the cell with Tuffy and Gregg while he made some phone calls.

Well, I've been in jail before and I know when you have to go to the bathroom you don't sit on the toilet with your ass. You take your pants off and stand on the seat and do an "oriental squat," so your ass is just above the seat. Well, I had to shit, so this is what I did, and I already had my shirt off, so I was naked.

Now word had gotten out, "The Allman Brothers were busted in Alabama," so even in this small town, a good size crowd had gathered outside. Every time they opened that door, the side door to the jail, all the people could see in the first cell. They were jumping up and down, trying to see over and around each other, and while I was taking my shit somebody came in the side door.

I said to myself, "I'm tired of this," so while all these people could see me, I came up and off the shitter like a wild monkey, and leaped clear across the cell from the toilet. I hit the bars halfway up, started yelling out and swinging like a wild monkey does at the zoo, staying in one place, but moving up and down and to the right. Now I got big cajones that hang down, and with my long hair and beard I looked and sounded like a wild man. So when I do this, the people outside shit and go blind. They start running around screaming. It wasn't too much longer when a lawyer showed up to ask us to calm down, and at dark they transferred us to another jail in the next town.

This was a little better, but they treated us like shit. There were white people in one part, black people in another, and that's where they put us — with the black people, which was fine with us. The white prisoners were whistling and making catcalls when we came in. That would have been trouble if they would have put is in with them, but the black guys treated us nice.

We spent two days there. They had bigger cells that would hold six to a cell and even bigger cells that were used as a bullpen. That's where everybody can get together, play cards and shoot the shit. Of course, the white guys got theirs, and us hippies and black guys got ours. About now we are all wondering about all of our dope in our suitcases and guitar cases, which are in the back of the truck.

In this jail you can send the trusties out to get milk, candy and cokes if you have money, and we have money. Willie's got a briefcase handcuffed to his wrist full of it, and he won't take it off because money was important to us. In those days we didn't have much. You did a gig, got paid, and used it to get to the next gig. Twiggs even killed a man because he wouldn't pay up. So you see, we believe in trying at all costs to keep our money. Now you understand why Willie won't give up the briefcase. However, he does take out money every day with Duane's permission, and buys candy and drinks for the black prisoners and us. Now this pisses off the white prisoners, but the hell with them. They treated us like shit. It was just a little non-violent payback.

Thank the big spirit we got out of there, because for some reason or other this black guy wanted to kill me. He said he was going to cut me up. I still to this day don't know why. I thought I was going to have to get down in the trenches with this guy, and I think it was Butch that talked to him and cooled him out. Which was good, because in jail you have to confront things head on and take your chances.

On the third day we were out of there, thanks to Brother Phil, and John Condon, our lawyer. Now John from Buffalo is a great criminal lawyer. He's the one who represented Twiggs in the Buffalo situation. But, no thanks to Charlie Court, who was Phil's lawyer in Macon, he sent a letter to the District Attorney saying he would give me to them and let everyone else go. Now Big Bro wouldn't hear that shit and he raised hell with Phil when we got home. It pissed him off. I was his horse even if I never won a race. I understand that there was some money under the table or something like that, and a nice piece of money I'm sure, but no matter. We walked out of there, and they were nice enough to give me a shot of penicillin that didn't work. I still had the drip.

I don't think I have to tell you we are all wondering about the drugs in the suitcases again. We are headed for Tusaloosa, Alabama, because we blew the gig in Jackson, Mississippi, which is where we were headed after the gig in Baton Rouge. So when we thought we were far enough down the road we pulled over and checked things out. No shit! It was still there. Right on top and not even moved. Kiss our ass, we couldn't believe this shit. Now we could get high, which we did. You name it we had it, ups, downs, smoke and even fly around. Finally we had a good night. Except I still had the drip.

When we got to Tuscaloosa the next day, I went to the doctor who gave me two shots and some horse pills. He says, "This will knock it out," and it did. But it also disabled me by gig time because I couldn't walk or sit down. My ass hurt.

Big Linda (B.O.'s wife), and Candy (his sister), came to the gig from Macon. Well, being that I can't walk, I went back to Macon with them, but after a day I felt good. It's my birthday and I can walk. If I knew my ass was going to get better so fast I would have stayed on the road. I think we had two gigs left, but I was home.

Being it was my birthday, I had some drops of LSD and dosed everyone that was there, Kim Payne and all the old ladies. The big house was rockin'. I was beside the house throwing up next to the goldfish pond. Nobody could see me from the road because of the hedge around the front and down one side, so nobody saw or could hear me telling God, "That's right wash my soul. Cleanse my soul. Get this poison out of my body." Then I went on and enjoyed my trip. I got with the spirit of the cosmos.

A couple of days later the band came home. I think somebody thought I went home early because it was my birthday. Duane asked me and I told him, "Hell no." I would rather be with him than any place on Earth. But I was here and made the best of it, and that was the end of that. Duane took me at my word. He knew I wouldn't lie to him. I thank him for that trust, and I'm proud I never dishonored it.

King for the Moment

A COUPLE OF MONTHS after the Alabama deal we were in Rochester, New York. It was chilly outside, not cold but chilly, and the gig was inside a gym at the junior college. The stage was made out of tables about two feet high with no barricades in front. The crowd was all messed up on reds and wine and really rowdy.

Twiggs was out front getting the count, the number of people there. Callahan was mixing, Kim was working stage left, and I was running stage right. During the gig something happened down in front of B.O. Someone pulled the wires out of the monitor. Well, I saw Kim go down to the front edge of the stage and say something to someone in the audience. The next thing I saw was Kim's ass being drug off this little piece of shit stage. I went running across the stage in front of the band, and dove in after Kim. At the same time Joe Dan came running from stage left and into the crowd. Now we have talked about this and nobody can say what happened, but right after we were throwing hands the crowd just picked us up and put us back on stage. No harm, no foul.

Everything chills out, and after awhile I'm sitting on a conga case against the back wall, almost on the stage right edge, the amp line was almost up against the wall, and you could just get by. I looked down to my right, and this gorgeous chick standing there looks up at me. When she did, she also licked her big red lips, and I just motioned with my right hand for her to come up. She was up in a flash. Even though she was messed up on reds, she was between my legs and undid my pants and down went the zipper. Well, I figured I wouldn't get hard in front of all these people, so I did nothing to stop her. She went down on me and my dick jumped to attention like a good marine. Elmoe, the pretty dick that he is, did not let me down. I looked over at Joe Dan and Kim with my mouth open, like can you believe this shit? Then this beautiful creature got me off.

Of course one of the great spotlight operators saw this. He didn't see anything else the whole show but picked up on this. Great! You know what happened next. He got this big white light right on me, and everyone in the building saw it. So what the heck, I'm king for the moment.

Joe Dan was watching the equipment after the gig while we were waiting to pack up, so me, Mike and Kim took this chick, or should I say she took us behind the building near three or four dirt piles and did her thing with us. She had such a good rose we wanted to take her on the road with us.

After we finished we walked around the building and the show had ended. People were moving all around us, and I heard someone call her name. I looked up and there is this older guy, her dad, standing right there. She stopped right in front of him and I never looked his or her way. I just kept right on walking into the crowd and made a beeline for the rear. We loaded up and got the hell out of there, and Joe Dan was bummed because he didn't get any. Once again we left town on the run.

Hell, that's the way we left Jacksonville, Florida, headed for Macon in the very beginning — on the run. So we are good at getting out of town on the sly or on the duff. And we damn sure knew not to get caught by some young girl's dad like Twiggs did in Birmingham.

This little young thing's dad busted in the room when Twiggs was in the bathroom with his daughter. This guy kicks open the door to the bathroom, beats the hell out of Twiggs, and is gone before you can say jack rabbit. So, we learned the hard way, dads are very bad dudes when they are protecting their daughters. When you see them coming, I say, "Follow me, don't hang, go and go quick."

Very Special Ladies

I'D LIKE TO MENTION three ladies who are very special to me, my sisters Donna Allman, Linda Oakley and Linda Trucks. I remember when Duane broke up with Donna. We were playing one of our freebie gigs in Piedmont Park, where we used to love to play for nothing on Sunday afternoon. We didn't have any gigs and no money, so we'd go to Piedmont Park, set up and play for free. Of course there were a lot of ladies there as well. Just pick one out. No, they picked you out. They would just reach down and grab you, look you right in the eye and say "I want some of you." Well shit, you think I'm going to stand in the way of progress?

Well this particular freebie, I think Sam was there from Janice Joplin's group, Big Brother and the Holding Company. I remember me and her got messed up at the first Atlanta Pop Festival sitting back stage. She kept mumbling shit like, "This is where it's at Red Dog, out here with the people. Shit, them friggin' musicians sitting back in the air-conditioned rooms at the hotel don't know where it's at. It's right here with the people."

I mumbled something back like, "Yeah you got that shit right." And she was right then, and she'd still be right today. The people, that's where it's at.

Here's a little ego on my part, I've always thought of myself as a people's roadie. Hell, I used to let a hundred people in the back door, if that's how many were at the backdoor when the show started. I figured they didn't have money for a ticket or they would have bought one, or maybe the gig was sold out. Either way nobody was going to get any more money, so I would say come on in. I mean let's party, we're not in our grave yet. You don't have to do drugs or drink. Well, a trip now and then and a little smoke don't hurt, but you sure as hell can get some rose. The more the merrier. I believe if you have a stage full of good-looking women, and you got 50 up there you're bound to get at least one hoorah. But of course getting fifty women on stage with the Gestapo roaming around is out of the question.

It's A Beautiful Day was there, Flo and Eddie, and a few other bands. This might have been the next day after the Cosmic Carnival at the Atlanta Stadium, which used to be the House of Henry Aaron, my baseball hero along with Ted Williams.

There's one picture I've always had in my head and it hurt me inside. I felt the pain Donna had. I saw Duane say something to her and then he walked off with Dixie, one of the Hot 'Lanta girls. That's who he was living with when he departed.

I remember standing in Duane's house on Burton Avenue in Macon when the Fillmore East Album went gold. I asked him if the roadies were going to get a gold album too, and he said, "I don't know. I don't know what they do. I never got one before, so I don't know who all gets one, but if you don't get one you can have mine."

And Dixie hollered out from the kitchen, "But Duane, I wanted that."

Duane hollered back, "You didn't help earn it. He did," and shit right there he sealed me up. I would follow him till the end. No matter what. I mean that, and you can go to the bank on that one.

When Duane and Dixie went over that little hill I hurt inside, and I hated that. I just love Donna, but of course, I didn't have to live with her, that was between her and Duane. Just like Berry and big Linda, or Butch and Momma Trucks, whose name was also Linda. They were the First Ladies of the band and I hated that they all had to move away.

Linda Trucks was a little stronger than Linda Oakley and Donna. I mean she would speak out if I tried to run something by her and say, "Bullshit, Red Dog." Whereas Donna and Big Linda might say, "Now, Red Dog."

Big Linda was soft-spoken like Donna. She took care of everybody. She would make sure that everyone had something to eat. You would come in the big house late at night or early in the morning and she would say, "There's some chicken in the fridge, and there's some fruit salad on the counter." No, Brother Berry I was not the backdoor man. Big Linda was an angel. All I can say is, I still love my sisters and they will always be my sisters.

Last Night at the Fillmore

WHEN WE PLAYED THE Fillmore East we took New York City, and she is still ours, for we surely belong to her. One time we were playing with Elvin Bishop and Johnny Winter. Elvin went on first, and while he was playing there was a bomb scare and we had to leave the building. There was no bomb, and eventually they let everybody back in, but this took some time. While Elvin's band was in their second set, Duane and Johnny were getting high together, or I should say getting down and rapping. Johnny started complaining that he wanted to go to the hotel because it was going to be late as hell before they got out of there.

Brother Duane, being the intelligent person that he is says, "Shit, man. We will go on last if you want. You can play in our place."

Johnny said something like, "You don't mind? Are you sure?"

Hell yeah, Duane was sure. That meant we could finally play the Fillmore Allman Brothers style, and that's just what we did.

I remember the feeling; Johnny had just played, all his equipment was off, and the stage was empty. The crowd was so quiet you could hear a pin drop. I could sense the audience wondering what happened to the Allmans because Johnny was the headliner and had already played. Well in all my days at the Fillmore, I never saw the stage bare for that long. No more than twenty or thirty seconds. Like on cue, the audience was death in silence, and then it happened. As we were pushing the drum risers in place, one diagonally from each side of the stage to their spot center stage, the crowd went nuts. The place went wild. Chills ran all over my body, my eyes watered, and my head swelled up as big as the stage. I knew we were going to take New York, and the people were really there to see us.

The band started playing and kept on playing, and kept on playing. We played all night. That's right, and when they opened the door for the audience to go home the sun was up high in the sky. The light of day was damn near blinding. We had taken New York. We sent the audience home with peace and love in their hearts, Allman Brothers style. The next time at the Fillmore we were the headliners, never to have anybody play after us again, in more ways than one.

We also closed the Fillmore East. We were the last band to play on her stage the night of the closing. The Beach Boys raised hell with Bill Graham. They thought since they were the Beach Boys, America's Band that they should be the last band to play, but Bill said the Allmans are closing the Fillmore. That went back and forth for awhile until finally the Beach Boys said they weren't going to play, and Bill said okay, see you later. But, being true troopers of the road, they played the gig and we closed. We closed Allman Brothers style.

It was even on the radio. If you were outside you could hear the bands playing inside because they had all the doors to the Fillmore open. Plus you could hear the radios, and it seemed like every car had it on.

Sometimes during a long gig somebody would cover if you wanted to go get something, but you had to bring back something for them too. Well, I really wanted to hear what it sounded like outside while we were playing, so I went next door to get a bagel. Let me tell you, it was great. It blew my mind. Made you want to dance. Which is what I did all the way there and back.

If the band gets me up and moving my skinny little butt they are playing, and this night I was moving Allman Brothers style.

A Brother

I REMEMBER THE NIGHT Brother Duane went on ahead, I died inside. We almost lost Brother Gregg that night also, and I thank the big spirit for Brother Chank. If it weren't for him Brother Gregg would have O.D.'d for the second time. The first time Chank and Poochie saved Gregg, Dickey, Kim and me, and this night he saved Gregg again. This was a bad night, for the Beelzebub Curse was really on us. It gave us some good things and then zap it put our ass in a sling.

Gregg and Chank didn't know Brother Duane went on. They just knew he was hurt really bad, and Gregg didn't want to deal with the accident. Chank and him got off on some Duji, and he ended up O.D.'ing. Brother Chank shot him up with saltwater, poured milk down his throat and put a cold rag under his chin, but that didn't work, and Chank was freaking. He put him in a tub of ice water then shot him up again with two full syringes full of saltwater but nothing, so Chank headed for the door to leave.

There is an unwritten law among those that do hard drugs. If someone O.D.'s you leave. You don't do shit. You don't call anybody. That's one time you don't go down with the ship. You do what you can for them, but if it doesn't work, you don't go down. Nobody forced anyone to put a needle in their arm. We were dumb for that.

I lived upstairs over Gregg and just got home from the hospital, which was right behind our apartments, and like I said, Chank was headed for the door when I knocked from the outside. Chank opened the door and could tell by my face that something was wrong. He said, "Don't tell me," and about that time a voice came from the bathroom, "Don't tell me what?" Now Chank was sad, but happy as hell because Gregg was alive. Then Chank ran things down to me and the three of us sat up all night.

Chank was always saving our butts one way or another in those days. He worked shining shoes in the barbershop next door to Capricorn Studios. Gregg got his shoes shined one day, and gave Chank a pair of sunglasses plus twenty-five cents for the shine. He fell in love with us, and we fell in love with him. He is an Allman Brother. 'Til this day he's a brother.

Jaimoe, well, let's just say my man was known to nod out at stop signs and red lights. Shit, it was no surprise to come around a corner and there was Jaimoe nodded out in the middle of the road. Sometimes he would wake up and say, "Why is everybody looking at me?"

"Because you nodded out Bro," and he'd say something like, "No, I was just looking at this," whatever it might be. I'll tell you, the man was noddin' or I ain't breathing, but in those days we all looked after each other — all for one and one for all.

It seemed like Chank was always at the right place at the right time. One time Jaimoe drove his car up on the curb in front of Capricorn Studios and just nodded out. Chank happened to come by and see him, so he helped him get the car parked right and went about his business.

He still lives in Macon, has a good job, and he's doing really well. He's a father, and most of all like me, he's straight and has his act together. The band should have hired him and taught him how to roadie. He would have been better than some of the road people we've had.

Ain't Going Nowhere

IT WASN'T TOO LONG after Duane's passing and we are still into class A narcotics, but this night we ran into some real strong Methadone. When I say that shit was strong, this is what I mean. When I went over to where it was being sold and copped they said to only do a little. Now with Methadone you have to wait. You drink it, so it takes a little while. I took two big hits and hung out to make sure I would get off, and yes I did. I was getting off fairly well and being greedy, wanting to get a kick ass buzz, so I decided to take another big swig before I left. The next thing I know I was in the hospital with the Oak. We both O.D.'d. And the same night Lou Mullenicks, a drummer in one of the bands that came to live in Macon, left us. He O.D.'d on the same stuff, so you see this was some strong Methadone. It kicked plenty of ass.

Just like that opium did to Duane one night after we played at Vanderbilt University. It was a great gig but afterwards was a scare. We'd eaten some hearts, that's speed, during the show. Afterwards a friend of ours showed up with some opium, and Duane ate a big piece. His thinking was it takes more opium to knock down the speed high. And it did — out — turn blue, he was close to check out, and I'll never forget them bringing Duane out of the hotel room on the ambulance bed. He was turning blue, I mean blue, and my heart dropped. I sure didn't want to lose him. Once they got him to a hospital and did their thing he was okay, and we left the next day for another day on the road together. I loved being together. It made the hard times not hard, but fun. And we did have fun until brother Duane left. Duane was my hero, and I know I was his dog. I've said it a thousand times. I would follow him to the end of the world.

One time Kim and Mike asked for a band meeting, so we are all present in a room at the Holiday Inn in Charlotte, North Carolina, all ten of us. Kim was the spokesman for him and Mike, so he told the band that Mike and him needed more money or they would have to move on. We were all getting $50 a week, that's the band and the crew. Well Duane says, "It was nice working with you. I wish you well." Then he turned around, looked at me, and says right in front of everyone, "You redhead motherfucker, if you leave I'll come and get you and drag you back if I have to."

I said, "I ain't going nowhere. I'm happy." That's just one reason why Duane was my hero.

The Rope Man

WE JUST GOT HOME from a long road trip. Duane had been gone about eight months, and I believe it was a Saturday night in June with nice hot sunny days. Kim and I went to a friend's (Ricky's) house and copped some Duji. Then Kim went home to the big house and I went to my apartment, the stud pad. Once I got home I snorted up a bag. Well, this wasn't a heroin high, but I couldn't figure out what kind of shit it was. It was kind of like an up thing. Then Kim showed up at my apartment and asked me, "What the hell is this shit?"

I said, "I don't know."

Then we went back to Ricky's but he wasn't home, so Kim went back home. Then Berry came by the apartment, and by this time I was starting to think maybe I was going blind. Kim had told Berry that I was out there just a little bit, and he came over to make sure I was okay. I told Berry I couldn't see too well, that things wouldn't focus, and he sat with me for about three hours, then went home. I was upstairs in the loft when this voice out front was hollering, "Red Dog! Red Dog!" It was Dickey. He was a little messed up, so we sat up and talked all night. Bluesky, who was Dickey's lady at the time, but not yet his wife, and him were fighting.

Boy, did that relationship go through some love and war changes. Like the one I just got out of about three years ago with Tracy Bush. Her and Bluesky were two wild women. There's something about wild women that sets you on fire. They don't make good wives, but in bed they can put something on you that Ajax won't take off and you never forget. They make you do crazy shit, like Dickey chopping up a Mercedes with an axe. I'd be saying something like, "You might fuck, but you won't fuck in this car again." Just like I was saying when I came home unexpectedly about one in the morning and Tracy was out. I cut up all her clothes in the closet, the sheets, and the mattress saying, "You ain't fuckin' on this bed no more." Like I said, they make you do stupid shit.

While Dickey and I were talking I was getting a lot better. Things have gotten straight in my mind. I remember I was telling him what I thought it looked like when him and Duane were playing, both way down on the neck of their guitars two feet apart. I said, "It looks like you two are fucking," and he said, "We are." I know it was double bad when the Oak would join in and make it a three-some. Now you got six eyeballs bigger than saucers looking right into each other so close together they could smell each other's breath. You'll never see anything like this in your life, all three of them huddled in a circle, with their fingers way down on the neck playing intertwining riffs. That's what I meant when I asked Dickey. Oh Lord — Get back — Slap my ass — What a friggin' sight. Can I get an A-men?

After a while I felt a little better. I told Dickey I was going to whip the guy's ass who sold me this shit. So about nine o'clock in the morning Dickey and me went looking.

Ricky was home and I was ready to go to war right there in his doorway when he says, "I got that from another guy. I thought it was Duji too." He told me who he got it from, and I knew I would see the guy that afternoon. It was Sunday and everyone would be down in Central City Park. Most of the times there were local bands playing, and that was the hang out place on Sundays in Macon.

I took Dickey back to the big house, where he lived with Bluesky, and went back to my apartment. About two o'clock I took the Ford van and went to the park. I was standing there with Tuffy, Tony Townson, Sammy Calvin, and a few others, and told them about the night before. I told them I was going to kick this guy's ass, and they thought I was just talking. Well, about the same time the guy showed up riding shotgun with his buddy who was driving. They pulled up and parked about 25 yards from where we were standing, and never saw us. I did the two foot shuffle real fast and headed for their car. I approached the passenger side at a fast walk, turned sideways with my right arm up above my head like I was throwing a rope, and fired my fist through the open window and up against the side of his jaw.

Then I tried to pull him out of the car window, and of course I can't. So I opened the car door and tried to pull him out, but he has his feet up against the inside frame of the car door. I pulled once and no go. Well, I'm going to pull his ass out or else, so I gave a big pull. I didn't see Tuffy reach in and grab him and pull with me. I landed on my back with him on top. Immediately I go into my spider monkey act, like lightning I'm up and on my feet. He's trying to get up, so I helped. I grabbed him by his long blond hair and slammed his face down on my right knee while bringing my right knee up to meet his face. I did this twice then stood him up and put another rope man swing on his ass. Except this time I popped him right in his mouth and the tip of his nose. Blood was everywhere, and it was a little embarrassing.

Everyone was watching and I was this peace and love freak. Well fuck it, I couldn't be that right now. The guy put me through a bad night and he deserved worse. I made him get in the van, took him home, and made him give me my money back, plus three bags of Duji. He swore it was the real stuff, and it was good as I found out on my way back to the park when I snorted up a bag. I wouldn't let that asshole ride back. Walk motherfucker, and you are lucky to be doing that.

When I got back to the park the fellows had already put a new nickname on me, "Rope Man."

Grant's Lounge

GRANT'S LOUNGE WAS DOWN on Poplar Street between Second and Third. It was the place to be seen in Macon. But it didn't start that way, it wasn't doing what I would call a good business, but Grant made a living.

It was a club that blacks went to for the most part. Kim, Berry, Mike, Gregg and myself were the first ones from our group to go there. Right where we wanted to be, but hell we couldn't go to many places by then. A few more than in 1969 when the whites and the blacks whistled at us and treated us like shit. It was only the whites now, but that was in the process of changing too and quick.

B.O. had jammed a couple of times at Grant's before this, so word was starting to spread that the Allmans come in and play sometimes. One night we were at the bar, at that time it was a horseshoe shaped bar, and Berry was sitting to my right, Mike to his right, and Kim to my left. We were drinking tequila shots and the bartender couldn't serve them fast enough, so we were ordering about five at a time. Now we had probably downed about four or five shots already, and they were lined up five deep in front of each of us. So we started, we got down to two apiece and told the bartender to bring two more apiece. I don't think we got the last two. I remember turning my head to look at the front door behind me, as this guy was carrying Berry out. The Oak's hair, long as hell, was hanging down with his head tilted back, as the guy carried Berry cradled in his arms.

As I was looking, I was leaning. And, I kept on leaning until I was right on my ass — going in and out.

This lady friend of mine told everybody to leave me alone, and she carried me, that's right, she carried me outside to the street.

She was one hell of a good-looking Georgia country girl too. She was strong, but fine as hell with beautiful lips and eyes. When she got me outside she flagged down this young couple around 20 years old, and told them I was Red Dog, and asked them to give us a ride to my apartment. Well, the guy said sure because he knew who I was. They were just driving by to see if any of the Allman Brothers were there, and it just got better. Now they got to help her get me home.

When we got to my apartment on Orange Terrace my lady friend told them thanks. The driver asked if he could help, but she told him she could handle me. I lived in an upstairs apartment and had a loft for my bedroom, so she had to carry me up two flights of stairs and put me to bed. She woke me up the next morning with a favor and cooked breakfast for me. That was one woman I should have married. She could have taken care of me in all areas, and I mean all. To her I say, when you read this and you lay down to go to sleep for the night, hear my voice in your ear softly saying thank you and good night.

There were many more nights like that at Grant's Lounge, and they got even wilder. It only took a couple of months from that night and Macon was ours. We had her in the palm of our hand. We were big shots and our shit didn't stink. I swear.

One night I pulled up in front of Grant's on my Triumph, the Green Weenie, making my normal approach. I hit the brakes and turned the front wheel while letting the rear end come around to the right and stop, while still holding the bike straight up. I straightened out the front wheel and let her roll with the downgrade of the road until the back wheel barely touched the curb, when this chick I had never seen in my life was looking right at me. She wore one of those low tops with her hooters hanging out everywhere, and I looked at her, engine still running, pipes sounding good.

Still sitting on the Weenie I looked hard and cool. I pointed to her, then pointed to the back of my bike. She was on, and away we rode. We rode straight to the graveyard, to my favorite place right under the vampire tree and close to the train track, Bond's tomb. We were completely naked when it started to rain. This was great, and then all of the sudden it stopped just as fast as it started. Still naked we are laying around, as we smoked a joint and had a cigarette.

I stood up and she was on her knees when a train came by. One of the guys was shining a spotlight around and shined it right on us, then moved it off, until he realized what he saw and put the light back on us. Well she just arched her back and stuck that big chest up and turned her head to look right at them. I don't know if the guys in the train liked it, but I sure did. At least they had a show.

Well we headed back to Grant's, partied the night away, and I saw her a lot on the side. I can't tell you her name, but I know somebody in Macon is doing some thinking. I wonder who. Her husband is a lawyer, and she is still married to him. I'll tell you this too, now there are a lot of husbands thinking, because she wasn't the only businessman's wife running through the forest.

Chase the Green Weenie

One time the Captain of the Macon Police told me if he caught me he was going to lock me up and hide the key, but if I got away, he would buy me coffee in the morning. Well what does that sound like? It sounds to me like somebody wants to run a little chase, and I'm just the guy. I felt froggy, so a few nights later I left Grant's Lounge and headed for home. I didn't live but about six or seven blocks from there, and when I came out of Grant's, I made a U-turn and eased up towards City Hall, which sits to the left of a six point intersection where First Street, Cotton Avenue, and Poplar Streets all cross.

There were about four or five policemen standing outside, so as I got in front of City Hall I ran the red light and did a wheelie through the intersection while they watched. Then I put the front wheel back down and away I went. The chase was on. One of many, and I never got caught on what I called the midnight run.

The Green Weenie was light and fast. She was a 640 Triumph Bonneville with a 750 road kit and ET ignition. Four wires, one headlight, one K-Mart tail light, and me — a hundred and thirty pounds soaking wet. She had two big 400 tires on her for flat track, and she was legal for the street. She handled great, so I could ride any kind of terrain. I would cut through alleys and parks on the runs. Ran right up the middle of Coleman Hill. That was as clean a getaway as I ever had. I had two police cars on my ass when I came to the intersection at the bottom of Coleman Park, which was actually was the side of a big hill that the city made a park of years ago, but there was no place to go. If I stayed on Spring Street they would catch me because there were no alleys right there, so as I go to cross Mulberry Street I looked to my left, the park, and I was gone up the hill with my ass not touching the seat.

Standing on the foot pegs, but keeping low so I could handle the Weenie.

Halfway up the hill this couple sat up right in front of me. I swerved and missed them by about four or five feet and their eyes were as big as hell. I came out of nowhere and was gone like a flash. A few blocks away I killed the engine and hid behind an old house. I was home free. Another night on the run. Another night of just having fun.

Wedding Day

On October 11, 1972, I married Jamie Faye McKenney, that's Miss Bunkie, at the Lake Wildwood clubhouse. What a party, if I do say so myself. I set this thing up just right. I invited everybody I knew, and gave each person two invites. That way they could bring their running partner because I figured you could have a ball no matter where you went or what you did if you have your best friend, male or female, with you.

We had well over two hundred people there, and there sure was some good music that night. Musicians from the Allman Brothers, Wet Willie, Cowboy, and a few others played. Mike and Kim set up and tore down the equipment.

Miss Bunkie arrived late, and I knew she would. No way was she going to be left at the altar. I knew she wasn't about to show up until she heard I was there, so when I arrived someone called her. Then she made her entrance. She was beautiful, the prettiest lady I've ever been with, and I've been with some foxes.

I felt bad that night for I made a big mistake. The Reverend Buffalo Gerald Evens married us. I had asked a black preacher I knew at the time, but Miss Bunkie had asked the Buffalo, and I made the decision for him because he was an Allman Brother. He was a roadie for about five years, but didn't return after the break up in 1976. My heart was a little sad though, because I hurt Mr. MacTier's feelings and he went home. I can still see the disappointment on his face today. I should have used better judgment. Buffalo would have gotten over it.

Ed McKenney, Miss Bunkie's dad, didn't come. He thought I wasn't any good, but he came around once he got to know me and found that I was a responsible person. Like I said earlier, we are still close today.

Berry passed away a month later. He didn't want me to get married. It wasn't anything against Jamie Faye. He just thought I shouldn't get married. He told me I should be doing Red Dog things. "Hell, Augie," he said. "You got more roses than you know what to do with. Why do you want to get married?"

As it turned out it was good. The band was slipping apart and Miss Bunkie was a comfort. She was one hell of a cook. I mean the food looked and tasted great. She could lay out a spread with everything good and proper like she was feeding the president. She was very keen on etiquette. She never held a cigarette below her waist, and never walked with one in her hand. She either put it out or handed it to me to carry until we got where we were going. Little things like this made her twice as pretty and she had great posture, which showed off her beautiful figure. She was and is a lady.

The first time I took Jamie Faye on the road we were flying out of Atlanta. We were at the gate waiting to board, and Jamie went to the restroom. When she came back she was crying, so I said, "What's wrong?"

She said she was in one of the stalls and saw somebody wrote on the inside of the door; "Sabrina loves Red Dog." Sabrina was a girl I knew from Atlanta, and wouldn't you just know that Jamie Faye would pick the one stall out of all the restroom stalls in the Atlanta Airport that Sabrina had written in.

I said, "That was before I knew you and we went about our business."

Not long after that we started using the starship, a stretch 737, with Allman Brothers written on the nose, and it was big. The bar alone was as long as my living room, and we had beds, swivel chairs, a stereo, that's where I first saw Deep Throat.

We never did break the starship in right though. Here we had a plane that cost $3,000 a day at least just to sit at the airport, and we hauled the old ladies around when we should have loaded that plane up with the wild kind and partied up. But, the band was into the old lady thing of having them with us — no fun.

Thank You My Lady

DUANE SAID, "RED DOG when we get old we are going to sit in two rockers on the front porch and have a truckload of Duji with a straw from it to our noses." Duane didn't like needles. If you could snort it, ok, but no needles. He said, "Red Dog you will be the one to tell the story," and it looks like part of that is coming true. I am telling the story, but the heroin thing, I had to give that up. We all know that you can laugh and tell jokes about dope, but in the end dope makes people dopes, with the exception of medicinal marijuana, which I need regularly because of my hyper state.

Duane was clean before he moved on. It took me some time after Berry moved on before I said that's it. Doctors, Methadone, nothing worked, except this super fox from Atlanta that came down to Macon to see me. I was so high on heroin I couldn't get an erection. Now this lady is fine. She could walk in a room and your pole wants to point, but I was in limbo. The funny thing is I didn't give a shit until the next morning when she was leaving to go back to Atlanta. She stopped at the bottom of the stairs coming down from my loft to my living room, and turns her head back up towards me at the top of the stairs, saying, "Red Dog, you used to be a hell of a lay, but you ain't worth a shit now."

Well fuck me, I've been shot. Now I give a shit. The lady has just put me in my place. She hit me where it hurts. I start thinking she is long gone and that's all I can do — think. I've been left with my limp pole in my hand.

From the time she left until now I am clean, clean as a white fish. I cold-turkeyed. The first week was tough, but I kept saying to myself, "You dumb ass, you could have gotten off this shit long ago. Hurt motherfucker. Hurt. Remember what this is like." I said goodbye to a three year habit, so thank you my lady, thank you. I haven't seen or heard from her since that morning. That was about six months after Berry left, but she saved my life, for I think I would surely be dead. The sad and embarrassing part is I can't even remember her name.

Gold Tops, Guitars and Gretschs

WE WERE RECORDING AT Capricorn Studios in Macon during the time period when Chuck and Lamar were in the band. The entire road crew was different too, except for Twiggs and me. Larry Brantley was the guitar roadie.

Dickey had this Les Paul Gold Top he didn't like. As a matter of fact, he couldn't stand it because you couldn't get a good sound from that guitar. You died. He didn't know it, but the bridge was broke, and I don't know why Brantley didn't fix it. He just tried to get by with it and string it up hoping that the strings would hold the bridge in place, but they didn't.

I went in the studio and Dickey handed me the Les Paul saying, "I never want to see this guitar again," So I said, I'll take it. Then I took it home and that is where it stayed, at home in the closet until about a year later when Larry Brantley showed up at my house. Believe it or not, we were still in the studio, so he says he needs the Les Paul. Now I wasn't worried or in a rush to fix it I was going to do it later because it's my guitar now, but I told him, "Dickey said he never wanted to see that guitar again," but Brantley said, "He has to have it."

I told him, "Okay, but if Dickey says one word to me I'm going to tell him, I told you he never wanted to see it again and you insisted." I wasn't going to take the blame, because I know Betts, so I gave him the guitar and he left.

A little while later I arrived at the studio. I opened the door to go in, and the first friggin' thing I saw was Dickey standing just inside the door to the practice room throwing the guitar in the trash can as he looks right at me. We made eye-to-eye contact as I saw Dickey throwing the guitar in the trash, so I turned left and went into the lounge. I didn't want any part of this.

Well, I wasn't in there two seconds when the door opened up and there's Betts saying, "I thought I told you I never wanted to see that guitar again."

I said, "I told Larry what you said, but he told me he had to have it, and I told him I would tell you that if you said anything to me."

Dickey told me, "I never want to see that guitar again."

I said, "Can I have it?"

He said, "I don't care what you do with it."

I said, "I'll take it." Then went over, got it out of the trash can and put it in my car.

I fixed it once and he said it was better, but still not right, so I sent it to Nashville to the guy who works on his '57 Gold Top. The guy set it up just like the '57 Gold Top and it sounds great, so now he likes it now, but it's my guitar.

I also have a Gibson J-50 thin neck. They don't make 'em like that anymore. That's the first guitar Duane gave to Gregg, and Gregg gave it to me as a wedding present when I married Bunkie McKenny. He wanted to send me to Jamaica but I didn't want to go, so he gave me the J-50 instead.

Jaimoe gave me a set of Gretsch drums with an 18-inch bass, 12-inch tom and 14-inch floor tom. What a great sound. love those drums. Jaimoe had a friend of his velvetize them, but that deadened the sound, so he gave them to me. I took the velvet off and now they sound great again.

I suppose one day I'll sell the instruments to someone who can get some good sounds from them. Hell, I can't take them to the grave with me.

Watkins Glen

BUNKY ODOMS WAS BOOKING gigs, and one day I walked into his office and told him, "If you want to draw a lot of people and make a lot of money, book the Allman Brothers, the Grateful Dead, and any third band you want for an outdoors gig. We will draw so many people it will make your head spin."

A couple of weeks later I was back in Bunky's office shooting the shit and rapping with the ladies, when he asked me how Bob Dylan sounded for the third band.

I said, "Great," but it wasn't too long after that he told me Dylan couldn't do it, but asked, "How about the Band."

"Yeah man," I said. "Three funky bands, all three play good and give the audience their money's worth, no rip off."

Evidently Bunky had been talking to Shelly Finkle and they set up Watkins Glen, which ended up being the biggest rock show in the world. Well have you ever seen 600,000 people? Well I have and its one hell of a sight. I think there was something like 600,000 people there and 200,000 on the road trying to get there. I was told people just left their cars, cut off the engines, locked them up, and started walking. Said they could make better time walking.

The stage was one you dream of as a roadie, about 20 feet high, 80 feet wide, and 60 feet deep with 25 foot P.A. wings on each side. A monster stage. When you stood on it and looked out at the crowd you just saw bodies and bodies and bodies. The ground in front had a slight upgrade for about 200 yards then dropped off and a lot of bodies disappeared. After about another 100 yards bodies appeared again. It looked like a big funnel with the little end right in front of the stage.

We had delay cabinets (P.A.s) every 75 yards. The first row of P.A.s had two sets of full cabinets. The second row had three sets, and the fourth row had four sets. One hell of a lot of P.A.s. When the sound from the stage got to the first row of delayed cabinets, they would kick in, and so on and so on.

The Grateful Dead's roadies were great, I mean super. We were there (the crews) three days early, and it was great to see my buddies. We had steak every night, and all chipped in to help get the stage ready. Two big families getting together to party and musically knock the world off its feet.

As I look back, this gig has even more meaning to me today than it did then. It was the last time the Allmans and Grateful Dead played together. Another sad note for me was that Payne and Callahan got fired months before. Ironically, right after the Brothers and the Grateful Dead played RFK stadium in Washington, D.C., but that's another story.

Backstage at Watkins Glen was neat. They had a round above-ground swimming pool and trailers, a shitload of trailers. Speaking of that, I never saw so many outdoor toilets. A solid row on each side of the field as far as you could see.

There were more good looking women there, and I don't mean this to sound degrading, but it was like going fishing and the fish were running. You just throw your line in and pull out a fish. Well it was better than that. It made it hard to do your job. They weren't just flashing, they'd drop their shorts and touch the rose right in front of you, and that made it a hard gig to work, but I managed. Somehow I managed.

The only way the bands and crews could get to and from the gig was by helicopter, so I just stayed there for three days and nights. That held true to what Janis Joplin said at the first Atlanta Pop Festival. If you were back at the hotel you were messin' up, and I never saw the hotel except the day we left to go home.

There was not before, and will never again be a gig like Watkins Glen. Two days before the show there were at least 200,000 people. So what are you gonna do? Party. Of course, with the Dead and the Brothers, there was a lot of tripping.

The Dead came out the day before the show and played for free. They played about a four hour set in the afternoon, which was great. It made the trip a lot better, and there wasn't anything like tripping with good music. Plus it gave the crews a chance to check out the equipment, but at no time did the buzz get in the way of the job. The job stayed in the front of your mind at all times. You could just lock in and focus on the task at hand with acid and pot. Alcohol, heroin, and coke, now that shit eats your friggin' brain and would definitely mess with your performance. You thought you were doing great, but instead you were steady messin' up. It's because reefer makes you stop and think. You get a little paranoid, which is good in a way. Your conscious comes alive, and you want to make sure you're doing the right thing. On the other hand, alcohol makes you a dumbass, and you just plow right on through without thinking about things.

Show day was unreal. People everywhere. Look in any direction and you just saw people. It was like being surrounded. The Dead played first. They played a killer set for about five hours. Then the Band played. They came on and played for about three hours. They played during the transition from daylight to dark. I remember they started one song and after about eight bars into it they stopped. Well the saying for a performance is, "Never stop, keep on going," but they just stopped. Tempo is everything, and the tempo wasn't right, so Robbie just stopped and started the song over. Then stopped again, and started the song over once more. My mouth was open. This time the song was in the right tempo and they finished the song. Kicked ass.

I thought this was great. Don't do it if it's not right. This wasn't normal and I like things that aren't normal. Even when I lived with Alexis Lawn, an English lady, she told me all the time, "If you put 100 people in a room, 99 will see it one way, but you, Red Dog, will see it different." I also go for the underdog a lot, so being the radical I am I loved it when they stopped and started over, and so did the crowd. They knew the Band wanted to give them the best version of the song that they could give, and that's what they did.

Our crew consisted of Twiggs and myself, who were the only original roadies left, and Buddy Thornton on sound. Buddy was a great mixer, plus he could fix anything. He built our P.A.s and board from parts laying around in the warehouse. Buddy used to work for McDonald Douglas, and later went to work at Capricorn Studios where we picked him up.

The other crewmembers were Willie Perkins (our road manager), Larry Brantley (guitars), Mike Arts (sound), John Gyro Gilly (sound), and Andy Lyndon. Andy called cues for the lights and was damn good. Twiggs had everything written out in a book note for note, beat for beat, and word for word, but you still had to read it and call it. No easy job, but A.J. was a trooper. He was Twiggs's brother, so you know he had to be on top of it or Twiggs would be in his shit.

Howey worked for Ira Dicks, who now works in Atlanta doing stage work, and most of the time we rented lights from Ira, who had a light company. We used four trees with twelve par lights per tree. The last of this crew, but definitely not last in my heart is Rodney Groth, who was in sound. Rodney went on and to work for Kenny G., and a year or so ago he bumped his head on a light truss. Then a couple days later his head was still hurting him, so he went to the doctor and found he had a brain tumor. He passed away shortly after that. I will miss him and think of him often. May the good spirit of the hound be with him. This was the best road crew we had next to the original four. This crew won the best road crew of the year award I believe in either Rolling Stone or Billboard.

We came on around nine at night. The Allman Brothers Band consisted of Gregg, Jaimoe, Butch, Dickey, Chuck Leavell, and Lamar Williams, and they played their asses off. The drummers were like two snakes playing as one, and they were in sync on this night. When two drummers play together sometimes they don't know how to compliment each other. They each just play their stuff, but Butchy and Jaimoe fuck each other. They are so close, and play so well together that they can entertain you by themselves. The main thing is they listen to each other. Yes, they were in sync this night.

Chuck and Lamar were in the groove, Dickey was talking on Goldie, and Gregg was giving a sermon. This was a great night. I sat there and thought it can't get any better, but it did when the Grateful Dead and the Band came out and jammed with the Brothers, which took the gig to a level never achieved before, and one that will possibly never be achieved again.

It was a spiritual feeling, that you had to witness to experience, which is exactly what more than 600,000 people did. Woodstock was great, but I don't want to hear it over and over again. 400,000 people for a three day gig and I don't know how many bands. That was good, but Watkins Glen was three bands for a one day event with over 600,000 people, and about 200,000 people still trying to get there. That was the gig of all gigs. So be it written. So be it.

As I said earlier this would go on to be the last gig the Brothers and the Grateful Dead played together. I think the Dead found out Phil cut a percentage deal for the Brothers. Each band made the same amount, but being the smart businessman he was, and naturally looking after himself and his band, we got a better deal than the other bands. So we never played together again and that's a shame.

Over the years, I had been trying to get someone to book us and the Dead with no luck, but many years later I almost pulled it off. It was about 11 p.m. and we were loading in to play a Bill Graham show in Telluride, Colorado, a couple of months before Bill left this dimension. I was setting up Butch's drums when all of a sudden these hands came around my face and covered up my eyes. I heard in a disguised voice, "Who is it?"

Well, I couldn't guess, but after a few seconds the hands went away. When I turned around it was Bill. We stood and hugged for about a minute saying, "How are you doing? Good to see you." Then we rapped for about five minutes and he said, "I know you've got work to do. Let me get out of your way and I'll see you later."

After he left one of the stage people came up to me and said, "Red Dog, you must be really important. I've worked for Bill for a long, long time, and I've never seen him come on stage to find someone and horse around with them. Much less give out a hug like that."

I said, "I don't know about being important, but me and Bill go way back."

After I finished setting up I went down the stairs from the stage and Bill was walking across the lot, so I hollered, "Hey Bill, what's the friggin' deal? Why haven't you booked a gig with us and the Dead?"

He looked at me and said, "I just never thought about it," so I said, "We should be doing one. People would talk about that gig forever."

He put his hand up and said, "Say no more." Then he pulled out his little writing pad and started writing.

Now if Bill said it, that meant it had a good chance of happening, but if he wrote it in his book that meant it was going to happen, and he was writing. As he was wrote he said, "We'll call it the Red Dog Festival. And that's on one condition, you introduce the bands."

I said, "Hell yes, I can do that."

Unfortunately, Bill went to join my brothers in the sky shortly after this, so it never happened. As before, just like Duane saying me and Twiggs would get a percentage of record sales, and twenty acres of the 478-acre farm out in Juliet, Georgia, that the band was in the process of buying at the time of his passing, but he never put it in writing. Same with the Red Dog Festival, but at least I got a hug.

You know I might be the only person to ever leave Bill with no come-back also. On New Years Eve in 1974 him and John Podell ran across the stage naked during intermission of a Gregg Allman and Cowboy gig at the Fox Theater in Atlanta.

Well maybe two or three years later we were in Colorado doing a Bill Graham show when John Gilly (Gyro) was testing mics. In the course of testing them Gyro said something about the heat, and how a nice beer with a good head would be, with the implication being a reference to head. Well, Bill went bananas and started getting on Gyro.

Gyro said he was sorry, but Bill kept on, and Gyro said again he was sorry. He must have apologized about four or five times.

I was on the drum riser and I've had enough to begin with because I didn't see anything wrong with what Gyro said. Secondly, I don't know how many times he said he was sorry, so I hollered out, "Okay Bill that's enough. He said he was sorry."

You really don't want to argue with Bill. I've seen him at the Fillmore just raise hell over the mic with the audience. Which I used to love, and the audience loved it. New York loved and still does love Bill Graham.

Well here we go back and forth. Everybody on the stage and part of the audience heard it, and finally I got my lick in, "Bill that's not near as bad as you and Podell running across this stage naked in Atlanta. That seemed to be okay." That's where I got him. No come back, because there wasn't one. He just walked off mad, but knew I was right, and I'm proud to say it never entered our friendship.

Carnegie Hall Ovation

WHAT A NIGHT. ONE that I will cherish forever. I'll never forget that feeling.

I believe it was in 1974 during Gregg's first solo tour when we played the hall on my birthday, March 27. We were about halfway through the show and just finished playing "Dreams" when Gregg announced to the audience that he would like to call out the man who supported the Allman Brothers Band in the beginning when I gave my disability check. I also had a 1964 Chevy Impala that we ran into the ground which ended up getting repossessed while we were out on the road. They came in the middle of the night and took it.

Then he said it was my birthday and called me out on stage, "The Legendary Red Dog." Well, the fucking place went wild. I got a standing ovation at Carnegie Hall in New York City. Then when I got to center stage Gregg and I hugged. A good hug too, I could feel his love and I know he could feel mine. When this happened I don't know how, but the crowd got three times louder.

What a great feeling. When you think of all the great people that have walked out on that stage and here you are walking to center stage and the place is going crazy, it lifts you up off the floor and you float. Now when I walk into Carnegie Hall I get this rush all over again just like that night. I think I'm the only roadie in the world that got a standing ovation at Carnegie Hall.

I don't know why, but the people of New York City have taken a liking to me from day one for some reason. They've always treated me as a roadie with respect. I thank them and the I.A., the stage hands union in New York. It's my favorite place to go on Earth — The Big Apple.

The Ohio Guy

WE WERE AT A gig somewhere in Ohio. The stage was set up about eight feet above the floor at one end of the building. There was about ten feet between the stage and the seats on each side, and about four or five rows of seats that run around the building like a balcony, but only about eight feet above the floor.

During the gig this big guy got up on the back of the stage and was knocking things over. He was really messed up, and knocked over a Marshall amp, so Payne, Callahan, and me all hit the guy at the same time. He fell back and off the stage. Flat on his back on the cement floor. I started to jump down and he was getting up, so I caught myself. No way was I going down there. He stumbles off and we didn't see him again.

Then one day during the Enlightened Rogues tour he showed up at a gig in Cincinnati. He told the crew hanging out in the production office about the knockout. That he wanted to see the guy that knocked him out because it had never happened to him before.

Well, one of the crew came and got me. They were smoking. They thought he was going to tear me up, which is what they wanted to see, as I didn't get along with this crew. They all followed me to the office to see what was going to happen. I went in and introduced myself thinking I might have to go to war with him at any moment. Well, he started laughing and said, "I thought you were this great big guy." He thought I was 6 feet or so, and 200 pounds or more. I said, "No, it wasn't me by myself."

I told him what happened, and said, "That should make you feel better. At least it wasn't this 130-pound skinny ass red head by myself." Although I think I could if the pit bull in me came out. Well, we left the office together and I set him up on the stage with me during the show, and he went home happy and pleased.

Enlightened Rogues

THE ENLIGHTENED ROGUES ERA, boy did I hate that gathering. This was our third road crew. Twiggs and me were the only original roadies left, and the new members sucked.

It was a few years after the break up when Chuck and Lamar played in the band. Now, I loved that band. Chuck Leavell's solo in Jessica is unbelievable, but Chuck and Lamar didn't come back because they thought that they deserved a little bigger piece of the pie. They thought they were contributing enough to help keep the band on top. Which in my opinion they did, but the band didn't see it that way. They weren't going to give up something they strived to get, and Chuck and Lamar weren't there in the lean years so they weren't getting a bigger piece of the pie.

If it had been the musicians from Enlightened Rogues after the passing of Duane and Berry, the Allman Brothers would have died. Quickly fizzled out. Which is exactly what the Enlightened Rogues band did. We had Gregg, Dickey, Jaimoe, and Butch along with Danny Toller on guitar, and David Goldflies on bass.

We were in Miami recording the Enlightened Rogues Album. Twiggs was talking with Dickey and he thought the band should sign with Phil. His line of thinking was, "You know how to deal with Phil now. You just have to watch things," but the musicians were too messed up and strung out to care. They didn't want to watch, just play, get the money and get messed up, so the band told Twiggs he was a Phil Walden man. This broke Twiggs's heart. He killed for this band, and never thought of anything except what was best for them, and now Dickey tells him that.

Twiggs came to the room that he and I were sharing in this big house we had rented for the band to stay in, and he told me what Dickey said, and said Twiggs was quitting.

I told him, "If you quit, I'm quitting too."

He said, "No, Augie. What are you going to do?"

And Twiggs was right. I didn't know much else except playing sports and fighting a war, so Twiggs left and I was by myself. I was the only straight [clean from drugs] person in the whole outfit. The road crew didn't like me and showed it. I guess they were jealous because I got a lot of attention and they sure as hell didn't like it. They were like all roadies are today. They thought if you were a drum tech, you were a dumb ass. That's what the atmosphere was like, and well let's say it changed me.

The band didn't sign back with Phil Walden. Phil had a comeback gig set up to blow the roof off. He wanted the band to open at the Atlanta Speedway for a NASCAR event, but the band went with Steve Massarsky as manager. Like Twiggs, I thought the band should have signed with Phil. Steve was and is a good friend of mine and a great lawyer, just not a rock and roll manager. He may have been a little like a fish out of water, which was not fair to him. I think he was doing it as a favor to us. We opened up in Jacksonville, Florida, and couldn't sell but a third of the house.

Not too long after Brother Twiggs left he hooked up with the Dixie Dregs (Steve Morse's band) and was the road manager for them. He worked for the Dregs up until the day he was skydiving in Duanesburg, New York, and his chute didn't open. Three days later on Duane's birthday I said so long.

Twiggs told me one time that the only way to go is skydiving because you are free, and that's the way he went. Free and broken hearted. It was killing him that he had to leave the band, but his pride wouldn't let him do otherwise and see the band all messed up like they were. He was a perfectionist. He knew how to pack his chute. His timing was great, and I think he just didn't want to see the band like that any more.

I was just a happy-go-lucky person. Always laughing and being funny, a free spirit to be caged, but the Enlightened Rogues crew was on me so bad that I went into a survival mode. It was like if you put a pit bull in a cage with a bunch of chows. What do you think is going to happen? The pit bull is going to kick ass, and that's what I ended up doing.

These guys would get messed up with the band and tell them a bunch of stories about me. With the band messed up like they were, and things getting worse, they started believing them. They still may think I was the one causing trouble, but I wasn't. I was trying to survive, but I didn't.

Well, when that didn't work I went to plan B. I shared a house with the bass player and he kept screwing me over. I told him three or four times, "I pay half the rent. You have to give me some elbow room. On stage you say jump and I jump, but in the house it's not that way. You are a paid employee just like me." I thought about it for three hours beforehand, and I knew if I did, I'd get fired. Well, I did it anyway. I dropped him like a bad habit. Wham, bam, down and out. I knocked out the bass player and Butch fired me. Now I do have the satisfaction of Butch telling me later that that was the biggest mistake he ever made. Dickey also told me that he had "Rook" (David Rook Goldflies) bent over the hood of a car and was going to blast him, but he thought he might kill him. See things have a way of coming around sometimes. Not all of the time, but sometimes.

This is why I disliked the Enlightened Rogues shit. Later in the Enlightened Rogues Tour (after I got fired), the band fired Jaimoe. Berry's sister, who was married to Jaimoe at the time, was asking where the money was going, and she had Jaimoe asking questions, so the band fired him.

I don't know how you fire a brother, but it was happening left and right. There were six original members of the band and crew when Enlightened Rogues started, and three when it was over. The band was in left field and strung out. Strung out and couldn't get dry. The dope and the bad people around had all but destroyed them. Still, somehow when Gregg, Jaimoe, Butch, and Dickey get together they play music like you've never heard. Allman Brothers music.

Outside of the music, Beelzebub is kicking our ass. The mood and the atmosphere was a carryover from the last days of Chuck and Lamar when we had a bunch of other shady amateurs around. I mean the last year of that outfit was rough too. There was just nothing like the original ten, love, trust, togetherness, and tight. We were tight like a gnat's ass stretched over a rain barrel, and that's tight.

But, remember with fame comes separation, and that's what happened after Berry went away. It started after Duane left us, Berry slipped into drugs and alcohol real bad, and so did everyone else, but Brother Berry went out on the deep end. So deep that Brother Butch told me that we may have to fire him if he doesn't straighten up. Well hell. I'm thinking how the hell do you fire a brother? I'm dying inside. First my world was shattered when Twiggs did his thing, and then the bomb came. Brother Duane was gone and now this? What the fuck was happening?

I do believe Brother Berry was coming out of it. You see, you can get messed up with a sense of responsibility, but when you lose that, that's when you hit the deep end. I swear he was swimming back though. When we added Chuck on keyboards it put the fire back in him, but Beelzebub was close and striking again.

Berry was hanging out with the roadies because of the power struggle and the separation that was taking place in the band. Actually, the difference was Gregg, Butch and Dickey quit hanging out with us, but Berry stayed the way he was. He may have been messed up but he was a brother and tried to keep the family together. He just couldn't do it, and the family slipped, and the moneyhood was here.

Brother Berry had been out at Ronnie Davis's house and was coming home on his bike. He wasn't what you would call a good bike rider, and we all got nervous and worried when he rode. He didn't really know how to lean a bike in a curve, and on that sharp curve on Napier Avenue he didn't lean good enough and bounced off the side of a city bus.

I do believe because Brother Berry was of such good heart, that the big spirit in the sky took him so he didn't have to suffer though the heartache.

Lamar joined the band and things looked very promising musically, but were still bad as far as being together. We were going in all directions. Then not long after Berry went Kim and then Mike got fired. I was thinking, "Goddamn, is this shit ever going to stop?" I was thinking they were brothers, and the band should have sent them to rehab, but that would cost money. Maybe it was easier to fire them and get somebody else.

They were messed up on a two-day gig at RFK Stadium in Washington, D.C. John and Caroline Kennedy were there, and we were playing with the Grateful Dead. They headlined one day and we headlined the next.

There was this girl at the gig who was in the stands behind the stage. In the afternoon where everybody could see her, she took off all started dancing. There are a lot of people here, and everyone can see her. She was just dancing away. She's got a great body, and very pretty. I saw her about a year ago and she still has a great body, one of those that actually got better. And she is still very pretty, but very spacey. A space case. She was up there in the stands doing her thing when some girl took her a sheet and told her to cover up, but no way. This chick takes the sheet and makes a shawl out of it, and now she really starts to become the dancing sex goddess. Well somebody finally got her down and we carried on.

The next day Mike and Kim had a buzz, so somebody told the band, and when they (the band) got there they saw them fucked up. Tuffy also knocked out this guy who worked for Phil when he tried to come on stage, so

Phil and the band were pissed about that too. Kim and Mike being messed up added fuel to the fire, so all three got fired after the gig.

It hurt that brother Joe Dan thought they should be fired. He didn't hate them, but he never really got along with Mike and Kim. Twiggs thought like me. He thought the band should have sent them to rehab and stood behind them.

It was devastating to lose two more brothers, but all was not lost at the gig. Both bands were in town a couple of days early, so the road crews from the Dead and the Brothers went over to RFK to check it out. We could tell the stage wasn't going to be ready in time, so we all jumped in and helped, and the second night of helping we went and asked Larry, who was the promoter, and owns the Electric Factory in Philadelphia, to get us a hot meal. We were tired of cold cuts, but he said no. So we said, "We ain't helping build the stage anymore. We're going to the hotel." Well with that we got a hot meal catered in, and from then on, we put it in the contracts, hot meals. So that was one good thing that took place at RFK Stadium that weekend, other than music. Hot meals at gigs. The beginning of at least one hot meal for the road crews at each gig.

    Before this the only hot meals I ever got at gigs were from Bill Graham and Tony Rafenno, two of my favorite promoters along with Ron Delsner. Tony laid out the first hot breakfast in Chicago in 1971. Occasionally Bill would lay out some ferocious spreads you would not believe; lobster, steak, crab, fruit, and anything that goes with it. For a good old southern boy like me he even had a good old fried chicken leg. So all you new guys on the block, remember who got you that hot meal: Ram Rod, Sonny Herrd, Sparky, Stanley O. from the Grateful Dead road crew, and from the Brothers: Kim, Mike, Red Dog, Twiggs, Joe Dan, and Tuffy. Just a few of the roadies that were there to pave the road for you. We old roadies worked hard to get the benefits you have today, so enjoy them.

New Crew

AFTER KIM AND MIKE, the road crew was good, real good. It was the best next to the original crew. We formed a band. We set up in the music room one night at my house on Albemarle Place in Macon, Buddy Thornton on bass, Mike Arts on drums, Twiggs was on guitar and I also played drums.

This was a neat house. No down payment and moved in. Paid $227 a month thanks to Miss Bunkie's father Ed McKenny, who I respect to this day. He is a smart businessman. He had a friend in real estate, and that's how I bought the house at a steal. I paid $27,000 for three bedrooms, two baths, a kitchen, four rooms across the front, and a basement that was divided into two rooms.

In one of the front rooms I had a music room, and was teaching myself to play drums. I had my drums set up with two stacks of speakers (one on each side and to the rear), so I could hear the music and the drums without a headset. I never played with anyone, but I watched Jaimoe and Butch, and had been listening for about five years, so when we started playing I had an idea, but my body didn't. We played around and were just having fun.

We were playing "Jazbo's Jump." Twiggs was trying to write this song. It sound like "Momma's Little Baby Loves Shortnin' Bread," and Gyro was there. He was taping what we were trying to do, and we'd been over "Jazbo's Jump" about twenty or thirty times when it happened. Somehow or other we hit a groove. I mean a groove, it was simple, but it was a groove. When we stopped Twiggs told Gyro to play the tape back, but Gyro said the tape ran out before we hit the groove, and Twiggs said, "Yeah, somebody else was in this room. I didn't think it was meant for us to tape." We just sat in silence for about five minutes, then called it a night. That's how we (the Almost Brothers Band) started.

Later on we started testing the equipment by playing in the afternoons before Allman Brothers gigs, and when we got home we had a guitar player, Barry Richman from Atlanta, who would come down to Macon and play with us. He was a damn good player, but he had too many hot licks.

We had rented an old warehouse, which is no longer in use at the Willingham Cotton Mill in Macon. A big monster place. This is also where the Almost Brothers Band rehearsed, but in a different building. The Allman Brothers used it for about two weeks. We, the Almost Brothers, still have no name.

I believe we were down in Texas, and had finished setting up and started playing. By now we have worked up a few songs, and while we were playing this girl came up on stage. She asked Twiggs if she could play the piano and jam with us, and Twiggs told her, "We can't play. We're just having fun," but she said she still wanted to play, so he said okay. Since he was in charge of the piano rig, if she broke it, he could fix it. Well, this chick could play and she made her licks work with ours. In other words, she came down to our level to play and made us sound a lot better.

The next gig was in Los Angeles, and we had a day off to travel, but when we got to the gig to set up guess who was there? The chick piano player from Dallas.

While we were setting up she helped Twiggs with the piano by cleaning it up, and then we played. She could play and was fun to play with, so afterwards Buddy Thornton, Twiggs, Mike Arts, and myself got together and talked. We decided to ask her if she wanted to join us and we could give her a job helping Twiggs with Chuck and Gregg's rigs. We told her all we could do was feed her and she could stay with Twiggs in his room. Then when we go home she could stay at Twiggs's house.

It wasn't only because she could play, but is was also, and this was the major reason, because she was broke. She spent her last bit of money getting to L.A., and had come just to play with us. I always thought after we played with her in Dallas that Twiggs took a liking to her, and told her if she could get to L.A. to play with us, that would win me over. Well that's what happened, and now we had a chick in the band.

After the road trip, we went home and started rehearsing with Barry Richman, the guitarist. We did this for a couple of weeks or so when we decided to ask Barry to leave because he was too good to play with us, and couldn't come down to our level. Or maybe he just didn't want to. Remember back when I said too many hot licks? Well that's what it was. It was like sometimes we weren't there at all, just a bunch of hot lick, and that was 20 years ago. We talked to him about it two or three times, but it didn't do any good.

Of course, the diplomatic one, me, was elected to tell him, so I laid the news on him. He wasn't happy, he was very sad, and it almost made me cry, but there was no way this would work. He was just too good a guitar player for us. Just before this, we named the band. We decided to call it the Almost Brothers because Virginia Speed was with us.

Shortly after Barry Richman left we had the great fortune to somehow or other have David Trash Cole join up. Now Trash could sing and play his ass off and make it fit into what we were doing. It made us sound like a band. We still weren't what you would call a good band, but we are a band. We had our own material and Trash could write his ass off. Great songs, so we took him on the road with us and gave him a job as a roadie with the Allman Brothers (the band let us do this).

We had Almost Brothers Band T-shirts made up with pictures of five men in long johns, one woman in lady long johns, and our names on the back. I think we were in Alabama one day doing an outdoor gig, and after we set up for the Allman Brothers, we played.

The show was to start around 5 p.m., and around 2 p.m. we thought, hell a lot of the audience is here so we can't play. Now Twiggs says, "The hell with it. Let's play." So we did. Twiggs told them over the mic that we were going to be testing the equipment. That we were the roadie band for the Allman Brothers, and were called the Almost Brothers. That we couldn't really play, but we liked to have fun and try. Well, let me tell you, we were blown away by the audience response. It was great. After each song the applause got louder, and we got called back for an encore. The Almost Brothers were truly born.

After this we no longer tested equipment in the afternoon. We waited until about an hour an a half before it was time for the opening act to go on and we played. Actually we were doing a set too, and that was a show. After awhile the opening acts started to complain. They got to play 45 minutes, but the roadie band was playing longer. How much longer depended on what time the Almost Brothers started, but we never, I mean never, caused the opening act to go on late. We had our pride as roadies and we knew we were doing something other road crews didn't get to, so we weren't about to mess it up and cause the opening act to be late.

We were the only act to sell out Grant's Lounge in advance. We advertised on the radio, and believe it or not, this was a major event in Macon. Now you talk about being nervous. I was shaking. I think the audience was at least half full of musicians, and there were some big name musicians there: Marshall Tucker, Wet Willie, the Allman Brothers and so on. Plus all the nice looking people of Macon were there. It was so crowded inside that people were close enough that you could almost touch them with your breath. There were people sitting all over the stairs going to the upstairs rooms, and one girl (Letty) was sitting right beside me on the stairs. Her beautiful blond hair was almost touching my cymbals. I think she was letting me know she was there, if you know what I mean? I should have had my head examined because I ended up standing her up twice.

That was a great gig. The music wasn't too bad and the feel was good. The feel of the whole night was just great, really great, as Twiggs would say in his southern drawl.

At this time in our playing we could be jamming our asses off and bang, we could lose it. We freestyle jammed a lot in our songs, and the trouble with freestyle is sometimes you can lose the one. You know? 1-2-3-4,1-2-3-4. And we could do that (lose it) really well, but when we hit a groove, brother we would hit it. It was almost like Duane and Berry would come down for awhile and sit in. If you know what I mean.

We played our song "Compactor," our instrumental number, and we hit a groove. And that was the only time at that time we ever hit a groove on "Compactor." It was hard to play and had a lot of changes. Well, we were playing way above our heads and it happened. We lost the one. We had six different beats going, but somehow or another it all came back together. We didn't stop in a situation like that, just kept playing and listening our asses off. Well, after the show a few people came up to Twiggs and me and said, "We loved that jazzy thing you put in the middle of 'Compactor.'" We were just looking at each other and saying thank you, but our eyes were laughing and saying to each other, "Boy they don't know we fell on our ass."

Around this time, about 1975, the Allman Brothers didn't go on the road for a year and a half, so the Almost Brothers played around Macon and Warner Robins, and did free gigs in Central City Park in Macon. That's how we supported ourselves.

This was about the time Cher was around. One Sunday we are playing a freebie in the park, but the gig really sucked. The wind was blowing and you couldn't hear anything, and she never said anything but kind things about it. She always treated us with respect and kindness. For example, we ran an open stage and I usually sat stage right and Twiggs stage left in these two tall director's chairs that a promoter in Texas gave us. One had Twiggs written across the back and the other said Red Dog. Well every time we got out of those chairs someone would sit in them, so we always had to ask them to get up, but Cher never sat in my chair without asking. She would say, if I were up, "Are you going to be sitting in your chair or can I sit in your chair?" Well, whether I was or not didn't make a difference. She was nice enough to ask and I wasn't about to say no.

In 1976 we were back on the road (both bands), but things were getting worse with the Allman Brothers Band. It was more messed up than ever and trickling down to the road crew and the Almost Brothers. There was a lot of pressure. We were arguing among ourselves, and there was trouble brewing deep.

The only fight I know of at the time was between Dickey and Butch. In the bar of this hotel in Mobile, Alabama, some dump motel actually, Butch was being his arrogant sophisticated self when he was drunk, and Dickey knocked him out. Then a short time later the guitar tech was jonesin' for Duji and got up in my face real bad, so I had to fire on him. Well, as soon as I started hitting him he turned his back to me and bent over, but I kept on hitting. Somebody from the crew (Rodney Gyro and Mike Arts) jumped in and they said break it up, but nobody saw him in my face. They just saw him with his back to me, and thought I jumped him from the back. He was a pretty big boy and nobody thought that little me would jump on big ass him from the front.

A few minutes later I was bent over a drum case and out of the corner of my eye, I saw him come up on my right taking an upper cut swing. So light and fast as the wind, I jumped back and he missed. Then before he could bring his hand down I was on him like a tick on a dog. I got that line from my man Jesse "The Body" Ventura. He used it in the movie Predator, but the same thing happened. I laid a couple on him and turned his back to me again as I kept firing. Twiggs was there in a flash. He broke it up and told me, "Augie, you are one bad little motherfucker." I saw it that time, and nobody in that road crew messed with the Dog from then on.

The Allman Brothers being messed up was having a major effect on everybody around the band. Such pressure that we disbanded the Almost Brothers to try and relieve some of it. Twiggs and I didn't think it was right that we made up two jobs for Virginia and Trash. We wanted to put all of our earnings into keeping the Allmans together. That was the most important of all, but it didn't work.

We played one of those big derby parties the night before the Kentucky Derby, and the music was hurting. Not because of Chuck and Lamar, but the rest of the gang were in left field. Hell, all we could do at the time was party, and they couldn't even decide what songs to play. After the gig, Dickey slapped Gregg around because they were arguing and each one wanted his songs to get more attention.

The next day after we returned to the hotel from the Kentucky Derby, and meeting the great Howard Cosell, who I think made Monday Night Football interesting. Willie called and said Gregg and Scooter left town in one direction and Dickey left town in the other direction. That nobody knows where they are, so we went home never to play with Chuck and Lamar again. The band broke up and we all went our separate ways. Remember with fame come separation.

Now Dickey says he'll never play with Gregg again. Butch says the same, and Jaimoe was just going with the flow. Hard times, no money, and the need to play and get off would eventually change that. They all had good bands and they all sounded great, but no cosmos. No running with the spirits. No getting off, so around 1978 the Allman Brothers regrouped. This is the Enlightened Rogues shit I was telling you about. The band was fucked up when it broke up. Fucked up when apart. And fucked up when they got back together. They were just plain fucked up in left field. No, by now they were in the bleachers and had more back stabbers around them than ever. From the road manager to the head soundman.

So here we go with Beelzebub dead on our ass and we are not all for one, one for all.

Leaving a Mark on Me

Duane always said he just wanted to leave a mark that he had been on this planet. Well he left a mark on me. That is to stand by my convictions and they will always see me through.

We were going from Atlanta to play the Sunrise Theater in Fort Lauderdale, Florida. We were traveling on our day off. Being that Berry Oakley Jr. was going to join us in Fort Lauderdale, I had told Dickey I wanted to go through Jacksonville to pick Berry's daughter by big Linda, Brittany.

Brittany lived in Jacksonville with her boyfriend. It was a little out of the way, but Dickey said okay, so I had the crew bus go to Jacksonville. People were pissed and they didn't want to do it, but they didn't say anything to me. I just heard whispers.

When we got to Britt's she couldn't leave right away. Her boyfriend was pissed because she was going with us, so he said he was going to the store and wasn't back yet. I say, "Babe did you tell him you were going to meet your brother for the first time?" Berry Jr., and Brittany are actually half brother and sister, but what the heck? It was still the same thing to me.

So she said, "Yes, I told him, but he's still mad."

I said, "Well tell him to come with us. What the hell is one more."

She said, "He won't do that."

Well that was it. I did what I could to ease the situation. My next step was to knock the mother out for being such a prick. That's what I wanted to do, but this was Brittany's deal and she had to deal with it. It's the law of the land.

I'm starting to feel the vibes from the bus. They didn't want to take the side trip in the first place and now there's a delay. Well, I couldn't leave here without her if it took all friggin' day even if I have to walk the dog with everyone on the bus. Fire me, but we were staying until she worked this out one way or another because she said she was coming with us. Well, finally her boyfriend showed up and she smoothed things out with him, and away we went.

It was really great watching them see each other for the first time. How could you, even if you only worked for the Allman Brothers for just two weeks, not want to witness two of the children see each for the first time?

Speck of Light

I cry out, I cry out
Nobody hears my plea
Push aside to die inside
Left to stand alone
where has The Brotherhood gone

I cry out, I cry out
Nobody hears my plea
Where are the spirits that lead the way
Where are the spirits of yesterday

Surrounded by the times of the past
In a room full of darkness there's a speck of light
I must fight

Red Dog

POSTSCRIPT

By Tom Dowdle

I WAS FOURTEEN YEARS-OLD and living in Kansas City when I first heard the Allman Brothers Band. That was a big step for me after having to move while in my formative stages. Kansas City alone was a big step, much less finding the song "One Way Out." Then my parents brought home a brand new guitar that I stumbled around on trying to pick a few notes and learn a couple chords. I learned the riffs to "One Way Out," and after a while came to find a friend who was also learning to play. The first thing he did was play for me the Brothers and Sisters and Eat A Peach albums. He attempted to teach me the main theme to "Jessica" and a little slide. At fourteen years old it wasn't an easy task, and it's still not today. But being impressionable, I kept on listening and trying. Just listening to that song for the longest time. I still couldn't get it quit right. However, in finding the music of the Allman Brothers Band at that time, I find something else now.

Cut to twenty-one years later and three moves — one to the East Coast, one further south, and the year 1995. After hearing a radio ad for a local concert, "The Power and the Music, the Real Thing, the Brotherhood of Lights Liquid Light Show, the Allman Brothers Band," that was it. I was hooked. I'd been to literally hundreds of concerts in the seventies, but nothing in the world like this. After a slow start and gradual climb in intensity I was hooked. By the third song I was oblivious to anything else and hooked for the rest of the night. Hooked for life as far as that goes. That was the first time I witnessed the true power of music, one that grabbed deep and hung on.

Immediately afterwards I started searching, trying to learn all I could about the music and the band. With the newness of the Internet and email I was able to learn a little more. I made contact with other kindred spirits. Soon to follow were forty or so shows, a trip to Macon with great friends, trips to New York City and the Beacon with more great friends, trips on a bus, and everything else in between and beyond. In a way a refreshing jaunt back, or better yet, a refreshing new start, in more ways than one.

I'll never forget going to Mama Louise and Mama Hill's restaurant, the H&H in Macon, where the strangest thing happened. After a great couple of days of music, many laughs, a good meal, and a warm hello to us strangers from Mama Louise, we were about to leave with our souvenir menu. As we turned to head out the door, in a flash the menu flew out of my hands and was immediately given back to me, but not by Mama Louise. By this crazy, hyper, hysterical person whom I'd never seen. He snatched the menu, signed it across the front, handed it back, and flew out the front door. I thought for a minute, "Who in the hell was that, and what just happened?" "Give me back my menu." And it must have showed by the startled look on my face that caused my friend to say, "Man, you don't know who that was? That was Red Dog...."

Personal thanks are extended to the Allman Brothers Band, their solo projects, and their extended family for the incredible music, Kirk West, Kid Glove Enterprises and Hittin' the Note Magazine, Mama Louise, Hittin' the Web with the Allman Brothers Band, everyone at O'Neal Road in Raleigh for the family vibe, Chuck Wehmeyer, Rob Davis for proofing and editorial assistance, Steve O'Malley, Dale Boyer, Epitome Production Services, LLC, Doug Dowdle, Shawn Wray, and Ron Currens for the second edition editing.